RELATIONSHIPS
WITH
Purpose

To Katherine,
Thank you for inspiring
"How to Live Happily Even After"
with your wisdom in chapter 8.
I was moved & deeply value
our transcendent conversation
now in written form. Enjoy.

♡ Love & Peace,

Judy K. Hermon

RELATIONSHIPS
WITH
Purpose

SECRETS TO BETTER RELATIONSHIPS
AND A BETTER LIFE

Judy K. Herman LPC-MHSP
Author of *Beyond Messy Relationships*

BMD Publishing

Relationships with Purpose: Secrets to Better
Relationships and A Better Life

Copyright © 2023 Judy K. Herman LPC-MHSP

BMD Publishing
All Rights Reserved

ISBN # 979-8851180422

BMDPublishing@MarketDominationLLC.com
www.MarketDominationLLC.com

BMD Publishing CEO: Seth Greene
Editorial Management: Bruce Corris
Technical Editor, Layout & Cover Design: Kristin Williams

Printed in the United States of America.

DOWNLOAD THE <u>RELATIONSHIPS WITH PURPOSE TOOLKIT</u> FOR FREE!

READ THIS FIRST

To help you know your next right steps and increase your perspective, I've created several video teachings and resources including:

- ✓ Audio & Video Versions of Interviews
- ✓ How to Create Your Relationship Timeline
- ✓ Making sense of Challenging Conversations
- ✓ Roadmap for your next right steps
- ✓ And more

Download them all at no cost whatsoever in the Relationships with Purpose Toolkit. It's my gift to you. ~ *Judy K Herman*

To get the toolkit, go to:
RELATIONSHIPSWITHPURPOSE.COM

CONTENTS

ACKNOWLEDGMENTS

Writing this book was a very different energy than writing my previous book, *Beyond Messy Relationships: Divine Invitations to Your Authentic Self.* The first drove me to make sense of the painful and accumulated transformational experiences within the life lessons of two marriages plus insights of working with clients in my private counseling practice. All has contributed to this continual journey of discovering my true self.

This second book drove me into the personal quest to know my *vibrantly authentic self* beyond the messy relationships. Thus, *Relationships With Purpose*, shows us the *secrets to better relationships and a better life.* Keep in mind that this endeavor of making sense of my life and relationships is not just a personal quest for me. Rather, it's for you. It comes from my heavenly Father/Creator, who loves us deeply and is conspiring for us. This is a gift of divine love to us all. There IS purpose through our relationships for a better life.

I'm thankful for each of the sixteen beautiful souls who were among featured guests whom I interviewed on the first season of my podcast, *Better Relationships, Better Life.* Each of them graciously allowed me to take our verbal conversations into written form that make up the substance of this book.

With that, I'm thankful for Bruce Corris and Corina Ambrose for massaging the raw transcripts and my edits into a readable book format. When communicating my desires and questions, they listened and encouraged me. They were true partners in my re-massaging of the manuscripts.

I'm thankful for graphic designer, Kristin Williams who patiently iterated several ideas for the book cover. She's a true artist, gifted with perception and intuition. Along with her talent and creativity, I felt heard and understood by her. As a result, she captured the essence of this book.

Seth Greene and Market Domination, LLC have been like a well-oiled machine on the back end of production. When deadlines needed to be extended, they've been more than considerate and gracious. I'm very thankful for the kindest and most cooperative team ever.

It was my mom, Barbara Phillips, who suggested the subtitle for this book. And I'm thankful to my four grown sons and daughters, Candace, Carrie, Andrew and Steven (and their families) for their encouragement and feedback. To each of my grandchildren who influence me to leave legacies of love, I'm thankful. Ella, Marian, Witt, Adelyn and Ava's playfulness and zest for life inspire me to keep growing, creating, and writing.

INTRODUCTION

I love helping people achieve better relationships and better lives. It's not my job, it's my passion!

In fact, if you were hearing me say this instead of reading it, you would hear the passion in my voice. Hopefully it's coming across in print. Maybe this will help. I LOVE WHAT I DO!

It doesn't matter who you are or what your status is. You've experienced relationships with purpose. We are all relational beings. In fact, our developing brains happen in relationship from the time of our conception and birth. Then it continues throughout our lifespan here on this planet. Yet we experience limitations because of our own lens of how we see ourselves and our relationships.

No matter where you are right now, it's worthwhile to gain life lessons from your past, wisdom for the present, and insights for future relationships. These viewpoints are actually an exciting and life-long pilgrimage of appreciating, growing, and knowing your true self. I call this journey, *secrets to better relationships and a better life*.

Here's why it's intriguing! For example, your 16-year-old self has grown to the age you are now (unless you *are* 16). By the way, I have encountered clients in their 40's still holding onto their 16-year-old ways of thinking. But a 16-year-old *cannot* have the understanding of a 40-year-old. But the elder self has the ability to reframe the context of the younger self. It's kind of like putting a familiar piece of art work in a different frame and mat that brings out previously un-noticed qualities.

And we can all gain a different frame of reference from others outside of our own experiences. Even though we are all unique, we can find universal truths that resonate on deeper levels with our personal stories. Living out those truths launches us into a more vibrantly authentic life!

That's why it's so valuable to learn of the experiences and stories of others. We are exposed to what we can't see on our own. It's like what I heard from my mentor, Les Brown. "You can't see the label when you're in the jar."

When we get outside of the jar, it helps us get unstuck. We are able to have a more holistic view of ourselves, others, and our relationships. Then we have the capability of expanding into our most vibrant and beautiful lives. We can learn strategies and ways of being that enhance resilience and growth in our relationships.

Changing our mindset and knowing the secrets to better relationships and a better life is part of our human journey. Otherwise, we'll feel like Bill Murray's character in the movie *Groundhog Day,*[1] who woke up to the same day over and over again. It drove him crazy until he began to realize the absurdity of his same actions and thoughts.

We inadvertently play out our usual patterns from childhood into our adult relationships. As much as we try to avoid what we don't want, we actually co-create those similar scenarios from our early experiences. And we're not even aware. They may show up in romances or marriages. They may exist in parenting styles. Those familiar patterns can even present themselves in professional relationships with a boss or with employees.

Even though challenges show up, it's possible to get off the relationship merry-go-round. It's possible to discover your purpose, increase your objectivity, and move into a higher level of relating. Greater awareness produces a better life.

This is not my first book about relationships, but it is the first one I've done this way. I'm not the only one you'll be hearing from. Nor am I the only one sharing insights. This book takes a team approach. It features my conversations with relationship experts and entrepreneurial couples who have grown past their *Groundhog Day*.

This book will help you make sense of your relationships. It will raise your awareness about the various challenges and opportunities. I want to invite you into different ways of thinking. You likely will have some aha moments as you ponder your situation. That's why it's structured into four sections of "secrets."

SECRETS TO BETTER RELATIONSHIPS THAT LAST
SECRETS TO BETTER RELATIONSHIPS WITH CHALLENGES
SECRETS TO ENDING RELATIONSHIPS FOR A BETTER LIFE
SECRETS TO HELP CREATE BETTER RELATIONSHIPS AND A BETTER LIFE

More than anything, may you become more hopeful about your current circumstances. May you see how relationships you're in now or the ones you've experienced in the past, can give you wisdom and perspective.

When you're aware of the purpose of your particular relationships, you can choose resilient and growing ways of being you. Your openness to the four sections of secrets will show you a positive ripple effect on every part of your life. Plus, you can get past your *Groundhog Day*.

MEET JUDY K. HERMAN

Before you hear from the relationship gurus who will share their expertise in this book, let me tell you a little bit about myself.

WHY READ THIS BOOK NOW?

First of all, your authentic and beautiful life is so worthy of dignity, love, and respect. No matter what season you're in, we all have limited time and energy. Yet, relationships can distract us from what's really true. Or they have the potential for growing our resilience and alignment with what's true.

It was Mother's Day of 2020 that my beloved second husband who had previously managed his bipolar disorder said to me, "Judy, I need to go to the hospital." Now, if the average person saw this scene in a movie, they might think this was a rational decision. Afterall, he facilitated bipolar support groups, took his medication, and visited his psychiatrist and therapist regularly. But unbeknownst to me, and his caregivers and friends at the time, he was way out of tune with reality. The paranoid delusions became fixated and it was impossible to reason with him. *They* were after him. The hospital was the only place he could go to be safe. (See page 212 with Dr. Harville Hendrix about the chaotic brain in chapter 10.)

If you're like me, we try to make sense of our messes. We try to reason with our loved one. Or we look for who is responsible.

It's not just the imperfections and limited efforts of the mental health industry. In my opinion, the internal stressors added up beyond capacity from his previous coping skills. External stressors included brother-in-law's sudden death along with the entire planet's reaction to the pandemic. It likely was the perfect storm awakening the mental illness that had become dormant for a season. He went to the hospital and didn't return in his right mind.

Maybe you've experienced loss or gone through trauma. It's likely different than mine. But something happened that changed everything. It changed your lifestyle, your relationships, or your profession. Perhaps it even changed your status or what you believed was true. (See the section of *Secrets to Better Relationships with Challenges*)

For me, the loss was overwhelming. Yet, it was also a divine appointment. There's more to the story in my first book, *Beyond Messy Relationships.* Released in 2019, husband was my biggest cheerleader as I wrote. But in 2020 I faced the status of being a "twice divorced" relationship therapist after a total 40 years of marriage. And the whole world was facing delusions with the pandemic. Well, some might argue they weren't paranoid delusions. But on some levels collectively, we couldn't discern "normal" anymore. I wasn't alone. And neither are you.

Writing this book has been a personal healing journey "beyond messy relationships." With every interview, I felt energized.

After each dialogue, I walked away feeling a sense of camaraderie. Knowing my need for relationships, those conversations began to fill the gap of loss. Stories of the guests gave me perspective of a better relationship and better life. Some have made huge impacts on me through previous mentoring or by my reading their books at various seasons.

I imagine certain authors or podcast guests, mentors, or even therapists have filled gaps for you too.

It was Mark Lukach's book, *My Lovely Wife in the Psych Ward* that gave me hope during recovery from a previous episode. (See Chapter 4, *How to Love Stronger Through Mental Illness*) Katherine Woodward Thomas's book, *Conscious Uncoupling: 5 Steps to Living Happily Even After* helped me transition into an uncoupled life I'd never known before. (See Chapter 8, *How to Live Happily Even After*)

ORIGINS

We all have clues from our early childhood experiences that shape our passion and personhood.

For me, dating back a few generations, significant individuals in my family came in multiples of four. In other words, I am one of four children. Mom was one of four. Maternal grandmother was one of four and great grandmother was one of four. I have birthed and raised four children in my first marriage. There was a time I had four grandchildren. But now there's five. In essence, I've been saturated by relationships even before I was born. This pattern shaped my passion and personhood.

Not only have I been surrounded with intimate and personal family relationships, I've spent my entire career trying to figure them out. You could say that God put me on this planet with a life and curiosity focused on relationships.

This book represents both the uniqueness and universalness of various relationships.

INSIGHTS

We all have good, bad, and ugly experiences loaded with life lessons. Here's where some of my early insights began. I planned to marry high school sweetheart after completing my freshman year of college. Instead, we broke up. There was a bigger life waiting. Then I met first husband while completing my bachelor's degree. As with most young couples, we had seasons of harmony.

Becoming a psychotherapist is a second career. The first career was homeschooling four children in the context of a troubled marriage. The disconnect and lack of partnership in that three decade-old union took its toll. I felt like a single mom with the massive task of shaping four human lives in the midst of a messy relationship.

You might identify with me as I tried figuring out what my issues were. I kept asking myself, "Is it me?" (See Chapter 9, *How to Extract Clarity from Emotional Abuse*)

A huge turning point for me was facing a significant garment of shame. It was like a lead apron that the dentist puts over your chest to protect you from X-rays. Mine was a vest that seemed stuck to my skin.

When I realized that I was wearing that vest and that it wasn't part of me or my skin, I took it off. That was the beginning of significant awakening. As a result, I trained as a volunteer counselor through our local pregnancy center. In particular, it was counseling and speaking through the post abortion ministry that became the embryo of my calling. It was there I heard stories of others' emotional pain, secrecy and shame. And I also witnessed them shedding their lead garments.

The more I counseled and spoke publicly, the more I desired to learn and be more equipped. Plus, I needed to provide financially for my family. I ended up with two master's degrees and became a licensed counselor in private practice.

Then the first marriage came to a bitter end.

MARRIAGES & RELATIONSHIPS

You likely have gained insights in your life with major decisions and shifts. For me, throughout my counseling and speaking career, I saw up close and personal what it takes for couples and individuals to produce real and lasting change. I've seen it collectively as a keynote speaker to audiences and as a retreat facilitator.

When two individuals are willing to listen with empathy and really see each other, they are able to shed their weighty garments. They feel connection with the ability to hold each other emotionally and physically. Even years later, many have told me how supported they felt through their counseling sessions or retreat experiences. They've learned the process I developed in how to make sense of the tension and passageways of their growth.

Perhaps you identify with help you've received in the past. Maybe it was a speaker or counselor, or retreat facilitator who spurred in you what you know to be true.

It was a pivotal moment when I decided to specialize in marriage and relationship counseling. I was freshly divorced and struggled with insecurities and what we now call "imposter syndrome." It's common to doubt and question ourselves. In fact, it's rather universal whenever we choose to live a better life.

You may have asked yourself, like I have, *who am I to. . . .* (fill in the blanks.)

For me, the question was, would I have the credibility to counsel couples, especially after going through divorce? But I decided to become certified as an Imago Relationship Therapist. (See Chapter 10 *How to Create Connection Beyond Conflict*) The training was intense and extensive. I was still trying to make sense of the three-decade old marriage. The internal dialogue of my conservative theology met the tension of my growing humanity. (See Chapter 2 *How to Respect Long-term Differences*)

As a result, Imago therapy became the emotionally safe container for that internal tension. And there seemed to be some magical energy when I counseled couples. It was the trinity of three people in the room which felt like sacred space. In a sense, this magical energy happens collectively through group retreats and even larger audiences.

What a privilege to watch transformation happen right in front of me! My work with individuals and families as well as speaking is such a rewarding profession. I know of no other that brings such intimate X-rays into the human soul.

Each client, couple, or group have become divine appointments. I've come to believe that the human journey is designed for struggle, growth, and flow. (See Chapter 1 *How to Create Long-term Love and Flow*) Going back to the analogy, I realize how common it is for people to live with that weighted vest that seems stuck to the skin. With therapeutic support, it's possible for couples and individuals to take off their vests.

The resilience of my clients has given me the courage to show up and be real. They learn, as do I, to leave behind thought patterns and behaviors that have been stitched into the fabric of their vests. (See Chapter 11 – *How to Be Better Through Enneagram Insights*)

You likely have gained courage from others in your life. As with most of us, we experience seasons of transformation and trauma.

FROM TRAUMA TO TRANSFORMATION

In the privacy of what I call the sacred space of my counseling practice, I've heard the stories of high achieving empathic and intuitive women in people-helping professions. I've also listened to business owners, entrepreneurs, and people in the corporate world. Their relationship messes may have been different from mine. But there were also universal themes and patterns that emerged.

In a sense, we can get accustomed to the messiness of our lives.

While facing traumatic issues with some of my clients, the intensity of second husband's moods became draining to me emotionally. Every episode of trauma in the marriage created a shift in perspective. I saw gaps in the mental health system that affected me personally.

The darkness of my previous work as a crisis response counselor had presented itself in my own home. I longed for peace and a healthy flow of relating. (See Chapter 1 – *How to Create Long-term Love & Flow*)

For some, what looks put together on the outside is a façade of the internal emotional pain and unhealed childhood wounds. As a result, relationships suffer. Whether it is marriage, parenting, friendship, peer or team, certain patterns exist. The lack of awareness keeps the façade intact. (See Chapter 7 – *How to Heal Better Beyond Addictions*)

In using the analogy, those weighted vests are parts of the human condition. The divine invitation is to recognize it and take it off.

It takes trustworthy relationships to live in the truth. Our common task is to become shame resilient as we've learned from Dr. Brené Brown. The invitation is to embrace the flow and beauty of life.

INTENTIONS & BENEFITS

I wrote this book to uncover the wisdom of therapists, relationship experts, and entrepreneurial couples who have learned through their own journey of growth and resilience. It's not just a book about improving your relationships. It's about your unique journey as a human being who has amazing potential for co-creating better relationships and a better life.

This book will show you differences in relationships. You'll discover the ingredients it takes to make a relationship respectful, cooperative, and even fun. It will raise your level of awareness about emotional abuse. You may become more aware of a longing you've always had. You might increase hope about the possibility of a better relationship and better life. You'll be more aware of help that is available to you. Or you just might know for sure your next right step.

Whether you're looking for new ways of thinking, seeking support, or need to know how to live a single life, this book will cover all of that. I hope you'll flip through the chapters and find just the right message that resonates with you.

If you approach me a year from now and say, "Judy, I read your book," I hope you would finish the sentence by saying "…this book was the beginning for me. My perspective has changed. I now have the courage to _____. My life and circumstances are so much better now."

I want the conversations here in the book to be a catalyst for you to take your next right steps. May it be a turning point, or what I call, "a divine appointment," for you and your relationships.

It's my intention to show you a portion of the relationship journey through the guests featured. They too have shown us their struggle, growth, and flow. So, let's begin.

SECRETS TO
BETTER
RELATIONSHIPS
THAT LAST

CHAPTER 1

HOW TO CREATE LONG-TERM LOVE & FLOW

•••••••••

Conscious Loving
with Katie and Gay Hendricks

JUDY K. HERMAN

I'd like to focus on two of your books, *Conscious Loving*[1] and *Conscious Loving Ever After*[2]. Share how people can love consciously and why that's important.

GAY HENDRICKS

Our book, *Conscious Loving*, first came out in 1990. Then we wrote *Conscious Loving Ever After*, which focuses on couples at midlife and beyond. We worked with couples in their 40s, 50s, 60s, 70s, and a couple of them up into their 80s. We discovered what it takes to have a good relationship at midlife and beyond.

KATIE HENDRICKS

There is a lot of mythology about relationships and long-term relationships. One of the things we are taught is that after a couple has been together a long time, they get bored and stop learning from each other. We found the opposite to be true. A long-term relationship can continue to have the magic of discovering each other. It depends a lot on each person's commitment to creativity. That's one of the main things we discovered when we were looking at what it takes to thrive in a long-term relationship.

JUDY K. HERMAN

One of the myths of long-term relationships is that it's normal to get bored and stop learning from each other. But the truth is that they *can* continue the magic of discovering each other.

GAY HENDRICKS

We discovered early on that there are three big things that allow relationships to thrive. When people don't do them, their relationships dive.

First, you can tell the health of any relationship based on how much honesty there is. Are people speaking the truth? Are people withholding secrets? Is there good communication? The answers to those questions tell us whether the relationship has vital fluid moving through it or not.

Second, people in thriving relationships both take responsibility for stressful situations instead of blaming and criticizing each other. Chronic criticism is one of the main things that breaks a relationship.

Third, people need to operate in their genius zone. They need to feel creative and to get more creative every day in their relationship. After midlife, people need to cultivate a relationship with creativity that allows for it to grow. Life without creativity is boring.

JUDY K. HERMAN

Three necessities will determine whether a relationship thrives or dives. They are:

1. Their level of honesty which includes good truthful communications
2. How they both take self-responsibility rather than blame or criticize
3. How they both cultivate creativity by operating in their genius zone

Before going further, I'm curious about your beginnings as a couple. What did it take for you to get where you are now?

KATIE HENDRICKS

Commitment. When we first met, we recognized each other from across a crowded room and fell in love at first sight. Then we fell into appreciation and had great respect for each other. When Gay started talking, at first, I thought he was so funny. Then, I realized he was the smartest person I had ever met.

I was attracted to his consciousness. That is what we've based our relationship on. When I went up to Gay to ask a question when he came to give a workshop at my graduate school, I couldn't even get the question out because he delivered on being honest. He was thriving and operating in his genius zone.

GAY HENDRICKS

When I went up to her, I said, "I'm very attracted to you." She caught my attention and there was something about her. It seemed like she had a special aura around her. She was pure love. That was my first impression of her.

KATIE HENDRICKS

I still can't remember the question I was going to ask him because he made me forget it when he told me he was attracted to me.

GAY HENDRICKS

Then I asked her out for coffee but explained that I discovered how I mess up my relationships and how I operate in relationships. I told her I only wanted to be in a relationship where both people tell the truth all the time and are willing to listen to the truth from the other person.

I wanted to be in a relationship where both people took responsibility rather than blaming and playing the victim. Finally, I told her I wanted to be with a woman who was as passionate about her creativity as I was mine. Then I asked, "On those terms, would you like to have coffee with me?"

KATIE HENDRICKS

When Gay asked me if I wanted to have coffee on his terms, what I heard him say was that he didn't care about what I was doing. And that he wanted me to drop everything and move from California to Colorado to start this adventure with him. I heard that he didn't know what was going to happen but that he wanted me to be all in on the relationship. So, I said, "What about lunch?"

We had an open possibility in front of us that I had never experienced before. My entire life I had been truthful and interested in how life and consciousness work. I've always wanted to understand why people get along and what happens when they don't.

I had been in my own creative flow. I was getting my PhD while I was a dance and movement therapist. I was teaching at the school when Gay came to give a seminar. I had never met anyone who was interested in the same things I was. We decided to make this big leap. I came out to Colorado and left behind my work and my friends.

We started looking at what it would take to be in this relationship. We looked around, and when we got together in 1980, we had known only one couple with a good relationship. But then they broke up. We didn't have a couple we could model ourselves after. So, we decided to make it up. We looked at the best practices and tried them. Everything we've written about in *Conscious Loving* and *Conscious Loving Ever After* are practices we took from our daily lives.

JUDY K. HERMAN
In addition to commitment, all those items were there in your beginnings. Honesty, responsibility, and creativity were in place back then. How old were you two at this stage?

GAY HENDRICKS
I was 34.

KATIE HENDRICKS
I was 31.

JUDY K. HERMAN
Did both of you learn and develop your own level of

consciousness to be attracted to each other at this level?

GAY HENDRICKS
I had just figured out what I really wanted in a relationship. Before then, I was never clear about what I wanted in relationships. I finally figured it out after being in several difficult relationships from my teens up to my 30s.

I was never able to make a commitment. Now I know that unless you're committed, you don't have a prayer of a chance in your relationship. If you have one foot out the back door or are attracted to other people, the relationship isn't going to work. It only works if you're willing to make a full body heartfelt commitment to fully revealing yourself while your partner fully reveals themselves.

JUDY K. HERMAN
"A full body heartfelt commitment to fully revealing yourself while your partner fully reveals themselves" is language we normally don't hear. But relationships won't work otherwise.

Katie did you go through several relationships that showed you what you didn't want before you met Gay?

KATIE HENDRICKS
My mother used to say, I went through men like lawnmowers. When I could see a relationship wasn't working, I would leave. Instead of sticking around, I would move on.

JUDY K. HERMAN
Both of you were in your creative flow individually. Then you took big leaps of faith. When I was writing my book, *Beyond Messy Relationships*[3], I came up with an acronym for the word

AIR. "A" stands for awareness. "I" stands for intentionality, and "R" stands for the risk of growth. I hear those terms and themes in your story as well.

KATIE HENDRICKS

We have an article called "The Relationship Dance"[4] where we argue the basic rhythm of a relationship is getting close and then being individuated. We have the urge to merge and the urge to fulfill our own creative individuation. Being committed to your own creativity and bringing that juice into your relationship gives it fuel.

It's important to honor our needs for space and alone time as well as integration and our need to be close. People need to let their partners know what kind of attention they want to receive and how they like to give attention. Then attention can be given and received freely. Those two things work well together to create variety, deepening, and refreshment in your long-term relationship.

JUDY K. HERMAN

The basic rhythm of a relationship dance is the urge to merge *and* fulfill one's desire for individual creativity.

On a practical note, since you are a dancer, Katie, do you both dance together?

KATIE HENDRICKS

We find that free expression of your uniqueness is a great fuel source for relationships. Gay dances with his words and his mind. He makes up puns, jokes, and spontaneous songs. Those are also forms of dancing. The dancing rhythm of the words and beauty of his voice allow us to be creative and let our bodies fully participate. We aren't only trying to relate to each other through talking.

JUDY K. HERMAN

Dancing is more than physical movements. There are other forms of dancing which include the creativity of spoken and written words.

What are the difficult things or huge transitions you've gone through in your marriage?

GAY HENDRICKS

From the beginning Katie and I wanted to have totally integrated lives. There was no downtime because we were both fascinated with the same subject and that's all we were fascinated with.

KATIE HENDRICKS

When people ask what we do in our spare time, we say, "This is what we do."

GAY HENDRICKS

Learning to work together has been a tremendous factor on its own. It's like the Olympics of relationships. If you're able to go up on stage with Oprah Winfrey[5], be your regular self, and not freak out, you've figured out how to be your authentic self.

When we started out, Katie and I would work with six couples in our living room. And we would work with some people at relationship conferences. Once Oprah got hold of us and we were talking in front of 10 million people, that gave us a taste of wealth and fame which can put its own stresses on a relationship.

Fame shines a bright light on your relationship. So, we made a commitment to be authentic whether we were standing next to Oprah or sitting next to somebody at a bus stop. Our commitment to authenticity was very important to us.

KATIE HENDRICKS

When couples work together, whatever issues they grew up with tend to show up in their relationship. One of the things that showed up for us was competitiveness.

I remember when we first started doing workshops together. We would be standing next to each other, and Gay would start gesturing, which would make him come into my space. Then he would start speaking and go on and on while I was standing there thinking that I also had something to say. I remember asking him if he could give me some space because I had things to say too. And he told me no. He told me that if I had something to say, I needed to show up and say it.

At first, I was shocked and startled by this. But then I realized he was honoring my own power to show up fully. He wasn't asking me to make compromises.

I started to get more courage to speak up and say what I was thinking. And in the process, I discovered a pattern between Gay and myself. Gay is about the same age as my older brother. Growing up, my brother was called number one and I was called number two.

I had been showing up, doing the work, and helping Gay when I realized I could create a different relationship with my husband. Instead of seeing Gay as competition or as a brother, I saw him as my ally and partner. Because of that huge shift we were able to co-create and dance together instead of tripping over each other.

JUDY K. HERMAN
Relationship stresses (wealth and fame included) can actually help you identify core values such as authenticity.

Learning to work together is like the Olympics of relationships. It reveals ways you related in your early family relationships. When you're aware, then you can create a different way of relating with your spouse.

GAY HENDRICKS
A big shift for me in our relationship was when I got in touch with my feelings. I came into the relationship heady and more disconnected from my feelings than I am now. Katie has a lot of feelings. In the early days, we spent our energy trying to make the other more like us. Katie would try to get me in touch with my emotions and I would try to make her more logical.

KATIE HENDRICKS
That's when we discovered partners shouldn't be trying to change each other. Many people get into a relationship and think this gives them a license to improve their partner. Instead, we decided to appreciate each other rather than improve each other. We made a steadfast commitment to that and increased our level of appreciation.

We made a commitment to end blame and criticism. So, our exchanges are full and we know what's going on. There is no one to blame or criticize. There is only discovery, appreciation, and having a good time.

JUDY K. HERMAN

Doing life together showed you what doesn't work. Then you commit to a new way of thinking. Rather than trying to improve the other, you decide to end blame and criticism. You are tuned into core values of discovery, appreciation and having a good time.

Personally, it took me 40 years of marital experiences *and* my counseling career to realize you can't do for another person what only *they* can do for themselves.

GAY HENDRICKS

That's why creativity is so important. I am here to honor my own creativity and honor Katie's creativity. We are in a relationship where we both honor each other's creative passions.

I'm a born writer. I write for a couple hours a day. If that kind of activity isn't okay with your partner, or if the partner doesn't have something they are equally passionate about, that starts to be a problem.

The great developmental psychologist Erik Erikson [6] said, "After 50 years old, every moment, every breath you take is a choice between creativity and stagnation." Are you going to be creative, or you going to stagnate and keep going through the motions?

JUDY K. HERMAN

One person in the relationship cannot take that breath or choice for another person to choose between creativity and stagnation.

How do you help those who have a partner who has basically exited out of their own life? What is needed?

KATIE HENDRICKS

Everything we wrote in *Conscious Loving Ever After* is not only about sustaining, but it's about renewing your relationship. Continuous renewal is possible, so you're not recycling the same patterns.

It's important to have a willingness to discover and learn. Once you discover something new, integrate it in your life so you have more choices. It's important to discover new things instead of having the same interactions and expectations of each other.

We have practices in *Conscious Loving Ever After* that assist people in handling the business part of the relationship. Many people in relationships make the mistake of mixing in the closeness of their relationship with the business of their relationship.

It can be difficult to navigate who is doing what. So, we have the two 10-minute conversations that people can use. One of them is a business conversation to manage the business of their lives. And the other is a structure for a heart talk that allows couples to connect with each other at their deepest level. Then the purpose of your relationship becomes revealing your essence and showing more of who you are.

Becoming unedited with each other was an unexpected delight as was creating a palpable flow of new impulses and ideas. It feels like a picnic all the time. When you open the picnic basket, there is some great new stuff in there that is juicy, nourishing, and fun. When you let yourself have room for the business side of your relationship, then your connections can be about what you want to share and discover. Finding a poem, discovering a funny cartoon, and learning about the world fills the couple's emotional reservoir.

JUDY K. HERMAN

Rather than repeating the same patterns, it's important to keep on discovering new things in the relationship. Then you provide a way for couples to navigate the business side of their relationship while nurturing the deeper heart felt connections.

Some people might be skeptical of what you're saying because we've been taught that relationships are hard. Are relationships actually hard? Is it really hard to live with another human being?

GAY HENDRICKS

No, it's easy to live with another person.

We often make it hard by lying, avoiding taking responsibility, falling out of touch with creativity, and then taking our frustrations out on the relationship. We deal with that a lot with our clients. Usually, one of them has been blaming the other for something for a long time. Sometimes, the other person created violations.

To get through to the creative side in the relationship, you must stand up and take responsibility for what you've created. That will put you in touch with your creativity. The moment you acknowledge what you created, even if it created pain, puts you in touch with your raw creativity. That is the creativity we get for free from the universe.

KATIE HENDRICKS

We have lots of evidence too. It's important to remember that taking responsibility is *not* the same as taking blame. It's not about criticizing yourself. It's about reclaiming your creativity.

You must recognize how you've been using your creativity to create this complaint or make yourself the victim. If you examine yourself and are willing to ask yourself what you're doing to create this experience, you'll grow as a person and as a couple.

You should ask yourself what you could choose that would create more contact and juiciness in an open space where you both can be yourselves and share what you want to create with each other. Doing that will change everything.

When most people think of taking responsibility, they think someone was right and someone was wrong. That's a big game people play in relationships. When we started taking responsibility in our relationship, it freed up our creative flourishing. It was a huge shift.

JUDY K. HERMAN

It's actually easy to live with another person by being honest and taking responsibility for creating even painful situations. Does going straight to blame and becoming a victim stifle your creativity?

GAY HENDRICKS

Yes. For example, if a room was on fire someone might take some responsibility by running over to the fire extinguisher and using it. Another person's instinct might be to look for who is to blame for the fire while the fire continues to grow.

There is a big difference between taking responsibility and blaming someone. We decided to create a no blame zone in our relationship and eliminated criticism and blame from our relationship, which took a lot of dedicated focus for a long time. Nobody has said a critical word in our house in this century.

JUDY K. HERMAN

Eliminating criticism and blame from a relationship takes a lot of dedicated focus. How does that happen when dealing with negative influences outside of your relationship?

GAY HENDRICKS

The number one priority in our lives is the flow of our loving connection. Figure out your priorities, and then focus on them. It's been many years since we've had to do this, but if either of us feels any kind of glitch or block in our flow, we sit down and figure it out in 10 minutes. We discovered there are no relationship problems that take more than ten minutes to fix if both people are willing to fix them. Usually, the problem is getting the other person to be willing to fix it. That can take years.

JUDY K. HERMAN

You two seem to have a lot in common, but that isn't the case for every couple. How can couples handle political, religious, or other core differences that may show up?

KATIE HENDRICKS

We want to help people get in touch with what they really

want. That often involves going through their fears. I've discovered most people get caught in fear, so their brain turns their partner into the enemy. You go into your reptilian brain, and you leave your cognitive problem-solving brain behind. When you're afraid, you can't solve your problems because you're caught in your own little cave.

We have practices to assist people to move through their fear and be present. When they are present, they can make new choices and see their partners as allies. We might have different ways we approach what's going on, but we hold each other as partners and allies rather than as enemies.

GAY HENDRICKS

Polarities are an important part of relationships. For example, it's common for one person in a couple to be more rational and for the other to be more emotional. It's also common for one person to be controlling while the other person allows themselves to be controlled. Ultimately, relationships only thrive if both people are committed to the relationship while they are committed to their own growth. That's how to thrive.

If you feel stuck in a relationship, you should look at a few things.

- Are there times when you aren't telling each other the truth?
- Where are you two playing out a victim-persecutor drama?

It's easy to get stuck going around and around like a dog chasing its tail. When you have conflict with your partner, ask yourself why you selected to be with this person. There is usually a good reason for it. It's important to learn which old patterns are resurfacing in your relationship. When I ask my clients to think about this, many of their jaws drop and they say, "Oh, my daddy was just like that."

JUDY K. HERMAN

Polarities are an important part of the relationship. To thrive, it requires both to be committed to the relationship as well as their own personal growth.

KATIE HENDRICKS

Relationships are about giving and receiving attention. Humans need attention as much as they need food and water. But most of us don't let ourselves ask for the kind of attention we want. We help people customize their appreciation. We help them think about how they want to be appreciated. We help them discover what has the most meaning for them and what feels the best.

People have a lot of differences in the ways they like to give and receive attention. Understanding your attention economy is a very important investment that pays off. You're not doing what we call "fly-by loving." You aren't heading out of the door saying, "Love you babe," and letting all the extraneous things that happen in life interrupt that flow of attention. We made it a priority to give attention to the other *when* they want it.

JUDY K. HERMAN

"Humans need attention as much as they need food and water."

GAY HENDRICKS

There's a quotation from the Gospel of Thomas that I put in

my new book, *The Genius Zone.*[7] It says, "If you bring forth what is within you, what is within you will save you. If you do not bring forth what is within you, what is within you will destroy you."[8] That's why creativity is so important.

I worked with a successful dentist once, and he loved to write poetry, but hadn't written any since he was young. He even won a poetry contest when he was a kid, but his father was a dentist, so he became a dentist. He started writing poems again at my suggestion and experienced a rebirth. He fell in love with being a dentist again.

JUDY K HERMAN:
What advice do you have for people who are experiencing pain in their relationship?

GAY HENDRICKS
At the end of our trainings,[9] we give out a wrist band that says "Breathe, move, love." This is to remind people when they are feeling stuck in their relationships to first take a few breaths. Then we tell them to move a little bit and change the position of their body. Then we tell them to love as much as they can from wherever they are. That's all that's ever required of us. Love as much as you can. Love yourself as much as you can. Love others as much as you can from wherever you happen to be.

SUMMARY

1. Three necessities determines whether a relationship will thrive or dive.

2. It's easy to live with another person when both are truthful, responsible, and creative.

3. Polarities are important parts of a relationship.

JUDY'S CHAPTER TAKEAWAYS

Just being with Gay and Katie has inspired me on a couple of levels. First, their energy made me want to start dancing again. Second, their priority on creativity emphasized to me (on a bigger scale) what's missing in our educational systems and corporations. Not only do we need this kind of flow in our personal relationships, we need to cultivate curiosity, awe, and wonder in every aspect of our lives. This includes how we relate as parents and how we show up in our careers.

The flow and creativity they showed us in this interview is what I call a "divine invitation." A question worthy of pondering is: "How can I nurture the creative flow in my life that brings aliveness to my relationship?"

I literally felt more energy after this interview. Gay and Katie oozed with beautiful creativity, and flow within that space between them. It's worth it to watch the video version of this interview included in your free Relationships with Purpose toolkit. Just go to relationshipswithpurpose.com

Gay Hendricks and Kathlyn Hendricks have been pioneers in the fields of body intelligence and relationship transformation for more than forty years. They've mastered ways to translate powerful concepts and life skills into experiential processes where people can discover their own body intelligence and easily integrate life-changing skills.

Katie and Gay have empowered hundreds of coaches around the world to add a body intelligence perspective to enhance fields from medicine to sports psychology, education, and personal growth. Together they have authored more than forty books, including such bestsellers as *Conscious Loving*, *The Big Leap*[10], *Conscious Loving Ever After: How to Create Thriving Relationships at Midlife and Beyond* and *The Genius Zone*[11].

Katie and Gay have appeared on more than 500 television and radio programs, including Oprah, 48 Hours, and others.

TO CONTACT GAY & KATHLYN

✉ info@hendricks.com

🔗 https://hendricks.com/

CHAPTER 2

HOW TO RESPECT
LONG-TERM DIFFERENCES

· · · · · · · · ·

Creating a Haven of Peace
with Dan and Joanne Miller

JUDY K. HERMAN

You both have made a huge impact on me personally as I've been mentored by Dan through his coaching program.[1] As we focus on respect and long-term differences, share about the beginnings of your relationship.

JOANNE MILLER

I met Dan on my first day at Ohio State. I was 17 and he was 18. I was beginning my freshman year, and it was his sophomore year. The rest is history. We got married when I was 19 and he was 20. It's been a journey. When I first met him, I had no idea what an entrepreneur was or a Mennonite, which is how Dan was raised.

I had a lot of learning to do, and I have done a lot of learning through the years. Dan is the wisest man I've ever known. I grew up without a father. I didn't have any brothers or other male influences in my life. Dan has always been my best friend, my mentor, and my psychologist. We've been married now for almost 54 years. We managed to go through all the ups, downs, and interesting curves of being married to an entrepreneur.

DAN MILLER

Our backgrounds couldn't have been more different. We were raised with different values and brought up differently. Any counselor would have told us that we wouldn't stand a chance, but we've embraced those differences in our marriage. We view our differences as bringing diversity and excitement to our marriage. We realized we don't have to be exactly like each other.

Instead of trying to make each other our clones, we examined our differences. It was an adventure to explore those differences which has given strength to our relationship. Because we came from such different backgrounds, we have to learn together. We got married very early, which we consider an advantage in that regard because we weren't set in our ways. That's been a wonderful opportunity for us.

JUDY K. HERMAN

Different family upbringings along with being so young is a lot to work through. How is it that you *did* marry as 19 and 20 year-olds and *now* have a 54 year-old marriage with smiles on your faces and a love for life?

JOANNE MILLER

It takes intentionality. We knew from the start we didn't want to emulate the home situations we came from. So, we drew a line in the sand while sitting in our eight foot by 42 foot house trailer. We decided we were going to start anew. We were going to put a new branch on our family tree. We've certainly done that in many respects.

Respect is what has helped us get through all these years, the moves, and the upheavals in our lives. Respect is always the first word that comes to mind, because we tend to lose sight of it in our marriage. We get too comfortable and expect too much from our partner without really respecting who they are, where they are coming from, and what their circumstances are.

The two of us are very different, but I respect and admire Dan for the strengths he brings to our marriage. I try to let him lead with that. On the other hand, however, I can feel so overrun because I am so different than he is. And he can easily put me under his thumb, and I will follow commands. But that's not respectful of him to not recognize that hurts my feelings. That's not my personality.

JUDY K. HERMAN
In order to respect each other's differences, it takes intentionality from both partners. Yet, some of us grew up in cultures where it's acceptable for the man to be the head of the household and have power over his wife. Did you two have mentors? How did you learn to balance that?

JOANNE MILLER
We had mentors and we read a lot. Before we got married, Dan left the Mennonite church[2] where his father was pastoring, which was difficult for him. I had never gone to church before. So, we started going to a little church in Mansfield, Ohio.

There we saw successful marriages that gave us insight to what marriage was supposed to be.

Neither one of us had recognized what a healthy marriage looked like until we saw people in healthy marriages around us. We were both so sheltered, so we were lucky to have these couples with families mentor us. We also read a lot of books, we talked incessantly, and we worked things out.

Dan and I are both in our 70s and we are still learning how to navigate each other. It's an ongoing road. And I must learn to speak up for him to recognize how I'm feeling. His personality doesn't lend to knowing what's going on in my head.

JUDY K. HERMAN

Curiosity and continued learning in a relationship is an ongoing process no matter how long you've been together. Dan, what was it like for you after growing up in the Mennonite faith tradition?

DAN MILLER

In the strict religious heritage I grew up in, they use biblical principles that say women are supposed to submit and be quiet. I had never observed anything other than that kind of husband-and-wife dynamic. It was clear, however, that Joanne wanted to have a voice and I wanted that for her too. So, we sought out mentors, we studied, and we went to coaching and counseling.

I've always viewed our marriage using my entrepreneurial lifestyle. When you find something, you figure out how to do it better, and the world rewards you for doing that. I've always seen our marriage as an entrepreneurial adventure.

It's not about hoping it works out. It's about being intentional. I want to be as intentional about making my marriage good as I am about making my business good. I constantly ask myself what I can do to make it thrive and prosper. It's not just a secondhand thing. It's very important to both of us. I don't give all my energy to my business only to give Joanne what's let over. We've never approached our marriage like that.

Joanne's always filled in as needed. But I've learned along the way not to force her into roles that fill the gaps I don't do well and assume she's going to do those. I must understand what she does well. She's an artist who is very committed to things she does in our community. She doesn't work directly in the business.

She's my biggest cheerleader and supporter. She wants to know what's going on. But she has no responsibilities because the things that need to be done for the business are not things that fit Joanne's skillset. I want to respect that. I have other people in place to do those things and allow her to be fully who she needs to be.

JUDY K. HERMAN
Intentionality is a crucial piece in nurturing respect and in managing your energy.

It sounds like Dan took a huge risk leaving his dad's church and faith. That's not an easy thing to do. What was it like changing your perspective, Dan?

DAN MILLER
My future was laid out. I was to go to school for as long as the state required and then quit to help my dad on the farm. That

was my responsibility. We didn't talk about the work I loved or the vocation I was called to do. I was supposed to do the responsible thing and step up and help my dad.

My choices for marriage were very narrow. We had a tiny church, and I was expected to marry somebody within the faith and within our little legalistic community. I didn't see that being realistic for me. I wanted more for my life than working on a farm. I wanted to see more and do more in life than farming could offer. I didn't find my options for marriage partners attractive in my tiny sphere.

I decided I didn't want to be confined by the farm. I wanted to go to college to expand my horizons, which my parents were not in favor of. I started dating girls that were everything my parents warned me against. It took a lot of fortitude to be determined to have a better life and exploring other arenas.

After I met Joanne, we met other couples who were driving nice cars, wearing fine jewelry, having a lot of fun in their lives, going on vacation, and doing exciting things all while being committed Christians. That spoke to us. We leaned into our mentors, who were people like that, early in our marriage and continue to do so now. We still look for couples we can model ourselves after and who we can learn from because this is an ongoing process.

JUDY K. HERMAN

It takes courage to break free from others' expectations. Finding mentors to guide you is key to growing a marriage that's different than what you're familiar with.

Joanne, at the beginning of your book, *Creating a Haven of*

Peace[3], you tell a true story about the gaps in your family of origin and the trauma you went through. Then you contrast that story with a life-giving story. Can you talk about how doing that has helped your marriage?

JOANNE MILLER

Perspective is something I teach and think about a lot in my art and my writing. It's something we need to be aware of in our lives too.

I can tell my story of how I grew up in a broken home, in poverty, on welfare, and with no father. I could go on and on. But there were things I learned through that.

It's important for people to look at their lives through different eyes and with a different perspective. Even though I had a lot of poverty in my life, I learned how to create beauty out of that. That's what I tried to do when I created my haven of peace, our abode, the place where we live.

JUDY K. HERMAN

How we focus on our past matters. We can have a different perspective that creates beauty out of trauma.

JOANNE MILLER

There were so many things I learned despite the circumstances that surrounded me. Sometimes it was hard. We can get caught up in our own circumstances that we don't see. Key questions in our marriage are:

1. What can I learn from this?
2. What does this make possible?

We do that instead of looking at everything negatively. We don't let that define us. That's not who we are or who we want to become. So, we had to figure out a way to get out of that.

This is not something Dan nor I were brought up with. It's something we are still learning. If we ever stop learning, someone might as well dig a grave and put us in it. That's part of learning to live together.

We had a conversation the other day about how people talk to each other, and how we communicate differently in our family. We talked about how on TV people are yelled at, point fingers, and accuse each other of different things. We don't do that in our household, and we never have.

Our children respected us enough to never do that. We didn't do that to them, and we didn't do it to each other. Everything wasn't roses all the time. We had disagreements. But we can sit down and talk without screaming, fighting, getting angry, walking out, or slamming doors. We don't do that in our home, and we don't watch that kind of TV either.

JUDY K. HERMAN

Life-long learning is part of our human journey. Questions like, "what can I learn from this" can help you get unstuck from negative circumstances.

A good mental diet is important. We have been surrounded with a lot of negative news, especially since the start of COVID-19. Our planet seems to be encased with a lot of negativity. What would be a good mental diet for a family with kids, or anyone else? How much news do we really need to know? How do you handle that?

DAN MILLER

As an entrepreneur, I want to know what's happening in business, what the trends are, and the opportunities. But I don't get helpful information from the news. The news is designed to share negative information. They produce these documentaries about topics that are divisive. They're training us how to hate each other and how to decide who is right and who is wrong. It's not healthy living, no matter what you're doing to create income.

We have a TV in our family room, and 99% of the time it has music playing in the background. We don't have regular TV access. We don't have news channels. We watch maybe two movies a month. We choose other ways to have positive, pure, and clean input. I highly guard my first two hours of the day.

One of my books is called *The Rudder of the Day*[4] and it talks about the importance of starting your day correctly. I guard my time when I get up and I go through my meditation, devotionals, and go walk outside. The things I do in that period of the day determine what I will get done.

I don't grab my phone before I go out. And our phones are never in our bedroom. We sleep when we're in our bedroom. I don't get up from bed to check my emails, texts, or the news. After two hours, I'm mentally prepared to start the day and we usually share a cup of tea afterwards.

JUDY K. HERMAN

Guarding mental time in the morning along with positive input throughout the day makes a difference on your productivity and connection.

JOANNE MILLER

We don't need to watch the news. We're going to hear it because everybody is going to be talking about it. We live in Florida and didn't even know when hurricanes were going to come. I know we're abnormal in that. I know there are people who say they've got to know what's going on. We can't do anything about it, though.

My favorite quote from *Creating a Haven of Peace* says, "Your success is not reliant on what's happening in the White House but is reliant on what is happening in your house[5]." Barbara Bush said that years ago in an interview.

I have the responsibility of my own family, my neighborhood, and my community. I cannot change the whole world. I cannot change the political atmosphere. I cannot change the weather. I cannot change all the things I don't have control over. So, I must concentrate on what I do have control over. And I can be content without ever hearing what's happening in the White House. That information would do nothing but make me angry, tense, irritable, frustrated, and depressed. I see it in other people, and I don't want to go there.

DAN MILLER

We haven't withdrawn from society, though. We're very active. We eat out all the time. Joanne's involved in community groups. I'm involved in men's groups. We travel a lot. We're very connected. We aren't trying to live in a hut in the middle of nowhere, but we choose what information we allow into our minds. We don't fill our minds with popular news stories, so we can live our lives full of intention and positivity.

JUDY K. HERMAN

Being focused on your areas of influence rather than on negative input helps fill your life with intentions and positivity.

Negativity can lead to depression and irritability which puts people in a state of suffering. When they're in a suffering state, they can't be in a creative state. That's why it's important for people to choose their mental diet as carefully as they choose the food they eat or the friends they hang out with.

DAN MILLER

I've been podcasting for a very long time and I'm fortunate to have a very large audience. I want to be able to share things that are going to help people live positive lives as well. I don't want to be somebody who's just passing along tips on how to see the negative, how to hurt others, or how to be disrespectful. I want to help them model the things that give their lives meaning and joy.

JUDY K. HERMAN

Yes, we all are influencing others with our own attitudes and values. What advice would you give to couples who own businesses or are in business together and are raising kids in a digital world?

DAN MILLER

People must control what their kids are exposed to. Don't give them unlimited access, information, and online connections because it's available. Technology can be used for a lot of things. It's like a brick. It can be used to build a cathedral or to smash someone's window. Many of the things we have access to today are the same way. If we use them properly, they can be great tools for good, but if we aren't careful, those same tools can be used in negative ways.

Parents need to control what their kids have access to and who they spend time with. The people they spend time with will be reflected in the people they become. Sometimes parents assume their children as little adults and give them absolute freedom. We don't think that is healthy at all. We want to be parents. We want to set guidelines and boundaries and help our children see things in ways that are going to help them be positive adults.

JOANNE MILLER

Being a parent doesn't mean being your kid's best friend. Somebody must be in charge. It comes back to respect. We always said we had a benevolent dictatorship in our house. Our kids learned the importance of being kind as opposed to being right. There are many alternatives to the digital world.

Last night we stayed up until 11pm playing games with our 26-year-old grandson. Today we have three of our grandkids in the family room and we're going to do an art project. There are so many things you can do that don't involve the internet or television.

We play a lot of games. I can almost say a day never goes by where we don't play something. I carry a deck of cards in my purse, so even at restaurants, we play games.

We do a lot of puzzles. We explore the area since we are still new to Florida. Recently, we took a road trip to see everything around us. There is no reason people need to be stuck in the digital world. It comes back to intentionality and knowing what you want.

You must set goals for your family and take control as parents. Our home was never a child-centered home. We were the parents, and we were in control, but we still did it with kindness and respect.

JUDY K. HERMAN

Parental control is balanced with kindness and respect for the children. You can have fun relating using games that don't involve the television or internet.

Do you have any advice for couples who have lost their spark? Some reading this might be jealous of your relationship. Some might feel like they are dying together instead of living together.

JOANNE MILLER

It's never too late for a new beginning.

Regret is pointless. That's not because I've done everything perfectly in my life. Regret just doesn't serve me because I know I did the best with what I knew and the tools I had at the time.

I could spend the rest of my life feeling guilty about the things I've done wrong. But that won't do anything other than destroy me from the inside out. That doesn't work well. I had a certain toolbox and a certain set of experience and knowledge at each point. I did the best I could. I never set out to destroy people, myself, or my home. Those tools and that knowledge changed in the different seasons of our lives.

JUDY K. HERMAN

What a powerful perspective about regret. Chronic guilt will destroy a person from the inside out. It's important to learn and have self-compassion.

DAN MILLER

Change is inevitable. Your spouse shouldn't be the same person they were 23 years ago. If change doesn't happen, there won't be growth. We welcome the times of growth and the ways we've changed. Joanne started to become an artist when she turned 50 after our children left home. She's developed a lot of what she knows today since then.

I didn't write my first book until I was almost 50 years old. We went through a tough financial crisis I created through some poor business decisions where we lost our investment. I'll never forget coming out of the hole after having zero net worth. Our monumental changes we've been through have given us opportunities along the way to embrace how we're growing personally and as a couple.

JUDY K. HERMAN

It's never too late. I love how you two reframe your "failures" as opportunities for growth. That makes for a remarkable partnership.

DAN MILLER

Judy, you and I both have backgrounds in counseling. We understand the dynamics of counseling. We understand the importance of gently looking at those early influences in your life and what framed you.

Now I coach people and we look at where they started and

where they are today. I don't focus on how you found success or failure. I want to focus on where you want to be in three years. My work is very future oriented. It's hopeful for people who feel like they've made some mistakes along the way. That's okay. Now, it's time for them to draw a line in the sand and decide where they want to be three years from now. That's a process people can use at 16 or at 89.

JUDY K. HERMAN

It's important to be grounded by gently looking at early influences. Then decide where you want to be in three years. You two have demonstrated that from your 54 years of marriage.

DAN MILLER

We moved recently, and many people wondered why we did that. They didn't understand why we would move several states away and start over. We love that sense of adventure and the opportunities that change can bring. Then we can reevaluate what we want to be committed to and how we want to invest our time. We've had a ball the past year and a half doing exactly that. We explored things together and anticipated what we want to do in the next 25 years. We are having a lot of fun making decisions because we intentionally created some major change in our lives.

Joanne, what do we say every morning when we get up?

JOANNE MILLER

We say we can't believe we live in paradise. It's a beautiful day in paradise every day. Even if it's raining, it's beautiful here. We love it. It's a great season in our lives and we are excited about it. Every time we've moved, it's been a new season of fun and adventure, because that's the perspective we chose to take.

DAN MILLER

It's important to add we don't just look to external circumstances to give us joy and peace. We'd be in trouble if that were true. Because everywhere you go, there you are. It's not like we moved and everything in our life became perfect. We love the environment and intentionally chose a lot of things about the environment. We chose where we live and the house we live in, but it's the life we live that gives us a sense that we're living in paradise.

SUMMARY

1. It takes intentionality to nurture respect and appreciate differences.

2. Regret is useless. Instead, look at the past with a perspective that creates beauty of out trauma.

3. Curiosity and continued learning is an ongoing process no matter how long you've been together.

JUDY'S CHAPTER TAKEAWAYS

This was such a refreshing time with Joanne and Dan Miller who have 54+ years of cultivating respect and appreciating each other's differences. It's no wonder that their grown grandchildren enjoy hanging out with them. Even through this virtual interview, I could feel the vibrancy of their interactions with me and each other.

They made courageous decisions to change their "branch of the family tree" and partner together to create their haven of peace.

All of our stories are different. And it's never too late to do the next right thing and create the life you want. Tune into the audio or video version of this interview included in your free Relationships with Purpose toolkit.

Go to relationshipswithpurpose.com.

Dan Miller is author of the New York Times best-selling book, *48 Days To The Work You Love.*[6] With over 140,000 subscribers to his weekly newsletter, his *48 Days podcast* consistently ranks in the top 1% of all podcasts. His 48DaysEagles.com community is viewed as an example around the world for those seeking to find or create work they love.

Joanne Miller has been a speaker at their live events and an integral piece to the success of their thriving 48 Days community. She is an accomplished artist, speaker, blogger, and author of five children's books as well as the co-author of *Be Your Finest Art.*[7]. Her most recent book, *Creating a Haven of Peace*, describes the decorating ideas, meals, games and celebrations that built her family's respect, laughter and lasting relationships.

Dan and Joanne have been married for over 54 years. They have 17 grandchildren and live in their version of paradise in Osprey, Florida.

TO CONTACT DAN & JOANNE

✉ dan@48days.com | joanne@joannefmiller.com

🔗 https://www.48days.com/
https://joannefmiller.com/

CHAPTER 3

HOW TO LAST LONGER WITH LIGHT-HEARTED LAUGHTER

· · · · · · · ·

Side-Splitting Humor
with Ken Davis

JUDY K. HERMAN

Ken, you're hilariously funny while making huge impacts on audiences as a famous comedian and storyteller. Share with us, who is Ken Davis offstage?

KEN DAVIS

As a skinny kid in high school, I discovered bullying. I could keep people from hurting me if I could make them laugh. If I could make a bully laugh when they were trying to hurt me, they would stop. We didn't become friends or anything, but my jokes would get them to stop.

Then, my English teacher encouraged me to use humor to affirm my worth and gain friends. During her class I made an inappropriate joke about the famous line in Shakespeare "Out damned spot," about the blood spot on Lady Macbeth's hand.

I suggested some other adjectives that could replace "damned."

It was horrible. My parents would have been astounded. My English teacher made me stay after class and she said, "Kenneth Alpheus Davis, look at me." I thought disaster was coming. Then she said, "Son, God has given you a gift, but you're using it to destroy my class. And that's going to change." So, she made me join the speech and debate team. My parents came to get me because she intended to expel me if my attitude wasn't right. Instead, she never told my parents, and I joined the speech and debate team. This began my career that has lasted for 50 years.

JUDY K. HERMAN
As children we learn how to move towards pleasure and away from pain. You had this gift, and it turned out well for you. We take the defense mechanisms we learned as children to survive painful places and trauma into our adult lives.

KEN DAVIS
For a long time, I equated my sense of humor to my self-worth. Finally, I came to a point where I wasn't giving speeches to receive standing ovations. I was doing it because I knew I was helping people. That made a big difference for me. Now I'm moving out of the public spotlight and living a more private life. I'm home more.

JUDY K. HERMAN
I'd like for you to share how laughter has strengthened your marriage. How did Diane and you meet?

KEN DAVIS

When I met Diane, she was peeling potatoes. At the time, we were attending the same college, and the university let us work to help pay our way through school. Both of us worked in the food development department. At the time, she had glasses with little wings on them. They fell off her face into the potato vat. She asked me to grab her glasses. So I reached to grab them while looking into her beautiful gray eyes. Then she said, "Give me my glasses."

I replied, "Only if you go out with me." That was the start of our relationship.

JUDY K. HERMAN

Was that impulsive? Or had you been watching her from a distance, and you worked up the courage to go talk to her?

KEN DAVIS

It was impulsive. I didn't know anything would come of it. But we got to know each other, and we got married a couple years after school.

JUDY K. HERMAN

Did she laugh at your jokes then?

KEN DAVIS

Yes, and she still does. But that might be so the people sitting around her will laugh and we'll keep getting paid. Could you imagine if clients looked at her and she wasn't laughing at my jokes? If there is a new piece that she likes, she lets me know. She has always been very encouraging when it comes to my career. I use a lot of comedy in my presentation.

At this stage in my life there are times when I forget what I'm talking about. I'll go down a rabbit trail and then forget what I'm saying. I didn't do this early on in my career, but it has happened quite a bit in the later years. It works out okay, because I ask the audience what I was saying. And they think it's part of the show. It's not part of the show.

If I ask the audience what I'm going to talk about next, that's a harder question they can't answer. Diane also lets me know where I can improve on my presentations. She's never done that in a way that makes me feel badly.

JUDY K. HERMAN

When she gives you advice, you are ready to receive it. Did you learn to do that? Early on in your relationship did you get defensive, and did she come across as accusatory? How did you grow into listening to your wife's advice?

KEN DAVIS

She gets frustrated with me and can become accusatory when I leave all the cupboard doors open or leave my underwear lying around. She wants me to close the cupboards or pick up my underwear and I don't always respond positively to that. Our 50 years of marriage hasn't been just singing and dancing.

JUDY K. HERMAN

Talk about how the pandemic changed your relationship.

KEN DAVIS

Everything I did ended at COVID. My lifestyle of coming home occasionally changed to being home all the time. We were together 24/7. COVID hit right as I was trying to retire. I was still doing some events, but I wanted to spend more time with my grandchildren. I wanted to be able to spend time with my wife. I wanted to learn what date nights were like.

I wasn't being good about fully following through with the transition. But COVID forced it to happen overnight. I learned that while I had been gone, Diane had become a very strong person. When COVID hit, we were living in Nashville, and there were so many COVID cases there. So we moved down to our vacation lake house where there were only two cases in the whole county.

We came down here to quarantine. While we were watching TV, the news said that COVID was going to be difficult for older people. Both Diane and I looked at each other and said, "Isn't that sad?" And then we realized we're 70. We *are* the older people!

One day while I was staring out at the lake, I said, "Someday I might be able to live here." My wife took that as an opportunity and sold the house in Franklin. Now we live down at the lake. She is so strong. She had an opinion and she expressed it. We talked about it, and now we live down here. Before we lived down here, we lived within 15 minutes of all our grandchildren, and we rarely saw them. Now that we live at the lake, they are here all the time with their friends. Some are college aged, and some are still in school. It has helped our relationship with our grandchildren and grown daughters.

JUDY K. HERMAN
Tell me about the different seasons of your marriage. What was it like to travel together? What was it like when you had young kids? Share some of the wisdom you have learned from your marriage.

KEN DAVIS

When I went on the road, people took care of every detail. I would stand up and do something and people would applaud. It took me years to realize I shouldn't expect a standing ovation when I came home. I expected that to happen. Instead, I would be met with, "Can you empty the garbage?" I had to learn to deal with that.

During this time of my life, I also learned I needed to realize how much Diane did. I had five people who worked for me as I traveled the world. And I had no idea what they did until they left. I was amazed by what they did. I had no idea all the things Diane did and the leadership qualities she had until I came home and stayed home.

When she had a hip replacement, I'm ashamed to admit, I didn't know how to run the dryer. I had to re-learn quickly. I told her she needed to heal quickly, or I might not make it. As I learned this stuff about her, it gave me an appreciation for her and what she did.

When we sat down and spoke with our lawyer the other day, I realized I didn't know the last time I had written a check or balanced a checkbook. She has done all the financial stuff. In preparation for whatever transition might happen next, she prepared a paper called "Getting the House in Order" that would help me if she passed before I did. And I've done the same for her.

JUDY K. HERMAN

How did raising kids change you? What was it like before you had kids? And what is it like to have an empty nest now?

KEN DAVIS

Nothing hurts a relationship more, (whether it's a marriage or friendship) than when one person in the relationship tries to perpetuate a perception of perfection. At first, I wanted perfect kids and I wanted to appear to be the perfect father.

JUDY K. HERMAN

Many of us can identify. How can we show up real instead of being worried about having a perfect public image?

KEN DAVIS

I tell people that just because I'm a perfectionist, that doesn't mean I'm perfect. It means I'm miserable some of the time.

I created the paintings hanging behind me. But no one has ever seen them because I saw a tiny flaw in them. I recently told a group of corporate people that they need to learn how to fail to accomplish anything. You try, then you fail. You learn from that, and you try again. I think some marriages end because one of the people in the relationship wasn't willing to try.

My children taught me the importance of being real and honest. In front of them I wanted to appear to be perfect because I wanted perfect children. I didn't create perfect children. However, I created children who hid their imperfections from me.

Years ago, in a survey, I asked young people what they wanted to hear their parents say. And the number one thing they wanted to hear their parents say was, "I love you." In the top three was, "I'm sorry I was wrong."

When I learned to apologize to my children, we grew closer as a family. I apologized for things like raising my voice or accusing them of something they didn't do. When I started doing that, I discovered my children realized forgiveness was available and that they could come to me and apologize. They stopped lying.

JUDY K. HERMAN

That is so healing. There are so many people who come into counseling who have the perception that their parents are perfect. They don't want to say anything bad about them. They want to maintain that they grew up in a normal and healthy family. Part of their journey is to see their parents as humans and realize that all humans struggle. Allowing them to be authentic is such a great gift.

KEN DAVIS

There is nothing better than for your children to know that forgiveness is available. That opens their hearts to the idea that God is forgiving and graceful.

JUDY K. HERMAN

A lot of people come to counseling and think their therapist has it all together. Many people go to seminars and think the person on stage has it all together. Why is it important for people to see each other as humans who don't have it together all the time?

KEN DAVIS

Portraying perfection on stage is one of the most harmful things a speaker can do. It puts a blanket of shame on people that they don't need to have. I tell stories because I think personal stories are funny. Someone once defined humor as a gentle way to acknowledge human frailty. When I share these kinds of stories with my audience, I receive emails and letters from people who tell me they have gone through the exact same thing.

Trying to appear perfect is terrible. For entrepreneurs admitting to making mistakes gives them grace and freedom. If you admit you've made mistakes, and make fun of those mistakes, then you allow those people to be more honest in their own lives. Everyone makes mistakes and understanding that allows entrepreneurs to work to correct them.

JUDY K. HERMAN

Portraying perfection is damaging and puts a blanket of shame on others. Humor is a gentle way to acknowledge our human frailty. Yes, admitting mistakes brings connection and well-being in our relationships.

Since we're being real, share how having ADHD (Attention Deficit Hyperactive Disorder) affects your marriage and your humor.

KEN DAVIS

Having ADHD has been positive for my career. When I'm on stage I think of new things, and they become a part of my speech that I use for years. People with ADHD think quickly and impulsively.

My ADHD has negative aspects too. My wife has to tell me to listen to her because I can only concentrate on one thing at a time. When I do, it only holds my attention for two seconds before I move onto something else. In fact, I thought I had Alzheimer's because both my dad and sister died from Alzheimer's. I went in to get tested and I forgot some of the things the doctor told me to remember. After taking the test the doctor told me I had ADHD, not Alzheimer's.

JUDY K. HERMAN
You were diagnosed much later in life and overcompensated for it for many years. You made it work for you.

KEN DAVIS
I had a hard time concentrating in school. It was hard for me to concentrate long enough to finish an assignment. Almost everything I did or tried to accomplish was interrupted by something else. I was afraid I had Alzheimer's because I would walk into rooms and forget why, which is a symptom of ADHD particularly when you're older.

JUDY K. HERMAN
What advice do you have for a traditional couple where one of them is out there in public? And the other is in the background, not getting recognized?

KEN DAVIS
The person who is out there all the time needs to know they are no longer a star when they step inside their house. Now they are a servant, a husband, a lover, a parent, or any other role they need to take.

Early in my marriage I would get impatient with my family's actions or their attitudes. Not because they were doing anything wrong, but I expected them to treat me how my fans treated me. When the person who is out there all the time comes home, they must change roles. People watching you on stage must see you as a human too.

Sometimes I show up early to my presentations and chat with the people there. It's not a performance. It's a desire to get to know people. As my life transitions, I realized I can use this gift in restaurants. I can go over to a table and talk to people about how beautiful their family is. This mortifies my grandchildren, but that's part of what makes life thrilling for me.

It's important not to perpetuate the perception of perfection. When you're speaking with others, whether they are your children, wife, or your friends, try to see yourself through their eyes. You must consider their position and not how offended you are in that moment. Try to see things through their eyes, so you can communicate. I'm an impatient person. That's part of my ADHD. I'm beginning to learn if I pause for a second and think about what they are thinking and going through, it makes a huge difference.

JUDY K. HERMAN

Being able to have an attitude of curiosity gives you some wisdom and gives you the ability to see the world through the eyes of another.

KEN DAVIS

It is important to learn the power of words. There are words that can be spoken in the heat of the moment that can permanently destroy a relationship. People should not solve issues over text or on the internet. You can't see the other person's eyes when you're on the internet and it's easier to say mean things.

People should look for the positive and reinforce it. I'll never forget my English teacher who didn't expel me. Instead she showed me that God had given me a gift. She opened the door to something I might never have seen otherwise.

SUMMARY

1. Portraying the perception of perfection puts a blanket of shame on others. Humor is a gentle way to acknowledge human frailty.

2. Be curious and see yourself through the eyes of your loved ones.

3. Learn the power of words and reinforce the positive in others.

JUDY'S CHAPTER TAKEAWAYS

This interview was filled with light-hearted laughter which I've come to believe is the best medicine! Ken was one of my first mentors to coach me on the craft of public speaking in order to get me ready for the stage. Not only do couples need laughter to last longer, we all do.

What I've learned as a professional speaker *and* as a counselor is that laughter puts a person at ease and eliminates defensiveness. This is what our families and marriages need. It's what our audiences and clients need.

Here's how this conversation touched me:

1. Keep increasing awareness throughout your life and identify what I call "divine invitations" (i.e. Ken's teacher who affirmed his giftedness).
2. Be willing to laugh at your own quirks.
3. Always keep on discovering God's grace, love, and support through your family.

Tune into the audio or video of this interview included in your free toolkit: go to relationshipswithpurpose.com

Ken Davis is a best-selling author, radio and TV guest, and one of the nation's most sought-after inspirational and motivational speakers. His books have received national critical acclaim, and he has been the keynote speaker for hundreds of major corporate and faith-based events.

As the president of Dynamic Communications International, Ken teaches speaking skills to corporate executives and ministry professionals.

He and his wife Diane, reside in Tennessee, near their two daughters and six grandchildren.

TO CONTACT KEN

✉ ken@kendavis.com

🔗 https://www.kendavis.com/

SECRETS TO BETTER RELATIONSHIPS WITH CHALLENGES

CHAPTER 4

HOW TO LOVE STRONGER THROUGH SEVERE MENTAL ILLNESS

• • • • • • • • •

My Lovely Wife in the Psych Ward
with Mark Lukach

JUDY K. HERMAN

I've felt such a connection with you, Mark since reading your book, *My Lovely Wife in the Psych Ward*[1]. It was in 2017, when I was dealing with my former husband's recovery from psychosis, that your book came out. We both read it and it made a huge impact. To me, it was like a divine invitation. Please share your story.

MARK LUKACH

By the way, I loved reading *your* book, Judy. And I'm glad to see that you're continuing to do work to help people move forward with their relationships, especially those who are impacted by trauma and mental illness.

Giulia and I met in 2000 and our story through mental illness started in 2009. We met when we were 18 years old and started dating after college. We had a fairytale romance. Then in 2009 an incredibly high-achieving, capable, successful career woman had an unexpected psychotic break. It was very serious, very acute, and lasted for a long time. It was extremely disorienting, and I felt really isolated.

2009 was over a decade ago and the conversation around mental illness and the terms used around acceptance and awareness were outdated. When Giulia had her first episode, we felt the stigma around mental illness. We thought that people who had mental illness were weak and taking medicine was the easy route. We had a lot of limiting and harmful mindsets towards mental health.

JUDY K. HERMAN
Yes, a lot has changed since 2009 with conversations around mental illness. I assume you hadn't seen it up close and personal until your wife's episode. Before this, did anyone in your life, family members or friends, have any kind of mental illness that you were aware of?

MARK LUKACH
When Giulia started to spiral and feel stuck at work, we had no frame of reference for what was happening. Neither of us had family members or friends with a mental illness. We were sheltered in that way.

As a result, we were woefully misinformed and ignorant about what treatment entailed. That also set the expectation that if she took the medication, in a couple of days she would be fine.

That wasn't the case, as her episodes can last between one to two months.

JUDY K. HERMAN

What you're describing is common. Even as a mental health therapist whose husband was going through this, I had similar expectations.

MARK LUKACH

As my wife's caregiver, I had to recalibrate my expectations. One of my expectations was the fear that I would have a patient as a partner for the rest of my life. I thought we might head in that direction because her symptoms were so acute and resistant to improvement from medication.

JUDY K. HERMAN

How long had you two been married at this point?

MARK LUKACH

We had been together for nine years and we had been married for three of them. Meeting someone in your 40s is different than meeting them when you're 18. We transitioned from being kids to adults together.

As many young people are, we were somewhat codependent on each other. We didn't know who we were as individuals, only as a couple. That was a huge thing we had to address. We had to ask ourselves what the codependency meant for our relationship and what the future of our relationship was going to look like.

JUDY K. HERMAN

In your late 20s, this is more than an intense journey in your marriage. Can you describe what Guilia's symptoms looked like and what was going on before all this happened?

MARK LUKACH

Giulia was always a high achiever. She had perfectionist tendencies, but it was never anything alarming. One time in college, she thought she lost a ten-page paper and was really panicked and upset. But a lot of students would get upset over that. She was always so certain of what she wanted and where she was going.

So, when work got really overwhelming, it was strange when she became hesitant and insecure. That's how it started, and then it escalated to physical manifestations. She would lose her appetite or wasn't able to sleep. And that quickly ramped up to her experiencing psychosis.

This all took place over about a six-week period.

JUDY K. HERMAN

She went from certainty as a high achiever to becoming hesitant and insecure.

MARK LUKACH

I am a teacher and this six-week period occurred during the start of my school year. I was settling back into the rhythm of school, which goes a million miles per hour. I had just left summer break, where I was at home relaxing. And now I had to have my head back in the game. The timing made it hard for me to wrap my head around things because I felt busy and consumed at work on my end.

When we got to the hospital and the doctors said the word

psychosis[2], I didn't even know what it meant. Since then, I've learned that it's an encompassing term. It often refers to disassociated thinking which is thinking that feels detached from reality. A person might have auditory or visual hallucinations[3]. It's rapid spiraling fixated thinking.

JUDY K. HERMAN
Psychosis is when a person loses contact with reality. They may experience delusions[4] which are false beliefs. Or they may experience hallucinations which are false perceptions involving the senses (sight, sound, touch, smell, taste.)

MARK LUKACH
Now we know that Giulia's psychosis was probably brought on by mania[5] because she has since been diagnosed with bipolar disorder[6].

JUDY K. HERMAN
Mania includes unusual high energy, excitable behavior, irritability, or extreme changes in moods.

MARK LUKACH
The mania explained her lack of ability to sleep and her constant energy. The problem was she was channeling the energy. And while I am unsure if she had auditory hallucinations, I know she had a belief system that was detached from reality.

She thought she was the manifestation of evil and that she needed to leave earth to cleanse it. She had all these other heavy-duty religious type beliefs that came out of left field from what I understand.

JUDY K. HERMAN

There are different spectrums of bipolar disorder. Bipolar I is the more severe category and can include psychotic features. But not all who have the diagnosis experience the illness at that level.

MARK LUKACH

The distinction is important for you to note because this goes back to 2009 when we didn't know the difference between any diagnosis. We didn't understand schizoaffective disorder, [7] schizophrenia, [8] or bipolar disorder.

There were all these other labels that were being kicked around by her doctors. I would talk to the doctor, write notes, and then get lost in Google trying to research as much as I could. I wasn't able to make much sense of it because it didn't square up to the nine years I had spent with Giulia up to this point. It felt like nothing made sense.

JUDY K. HERMAN

How long was she in the hospital the first time?

MARK LUKACH

She was in the hospital for 23 days and then she transitioned to an outpatient program. By this point I realized the severity of what we were going through. I took a lengthy leave from work. I basically took a semester off. I was looking forward to getting her home. But it was disorienting going from only being able to visit for 90 minutes during the day to being the only adult responsible for her 24 hours a day.

We come from loving and supporting families, but they live all over the place. During this time, we were the only ones from either side of the family who lived in California. My parents were living in Japan at the time and Giulia is from Italy, where her parents were. Having the ability to lean on family wasn't there. They were on the other side of the world and there were nine and 12-hour time zone differences to contend with. I felt an immense responsibility to take care of Giulia.

JUDY K. HERMAN
That's a heavy load for a 27-year-old man.

MARK LUKACH
I was still just a kid at the time. We had just begun thinking about having kids, and I was grieving the future I thought we were no longer going to have. I was doing all this privately because I felt I needed to project an image of optimism and cheer for Giulia. I was so scared and sad, but I had to keep that from her because I was worried about upsetting her.

I didn't know how everything worked. I thought my optimistic feelings could somehow be contagious and change her feelings. I thought I would make things worse for her if I had a bad attitude. It was an exhausting and draining time. The biggest difference between now and 2009 is that in 2009 there was no conversation around mental health or bipolar disorder.

JUDY K. HERMAN
In "normal" circumstances, optimism can influence others. And yes, mental illness is now getting more attention and less stigma than years past.

MARK LUKACH
I'm glad you said you found my book when you needed it.

When we were going through this, I was looking for a book that would help me. I was reading a lot of great and helpful books about what Giulia was experiencing. But I couldn't find one about what I was experiencing.

I'm a historian, a researcher, and a reader. So, I was trying to find examples of people explaining what happened to them, and to give me a sense of not being alone. I couldn't find any.

Through that sense of loneliness and isolation, and the realization there were other families going through something similar in psych wards, I realized there are so many people who go through the uncertainty, burden, and exhaustion of caregiving alone. That absence made me want to fill that void.

JUDY K. HERMAN
It's amazing that you were able to get a bigger perspective around all this, Mark.

MARK LUKACH
During Giulia's first episode, she spent about a month in the hospital. Her outpatient program was about nine months long and she was very depressed and suicidal. I actively worried about her safety at that time. Then they tweaked the medicine the right way, and we had this remarkable recovery where it felt like Giulia was back.

So, we hoped this was a one-off episode. That took roughly 10 months from start to finish. It was a long time and I had to go back to work. Afterwards, we hoped things were well enough that we could proceed back with the future we had envisioned. Giulia resumed working. We had a child together.

That was going well until she went back to work after maternity leave. Our baby was five months old, and she had a relapse. She was in the hospital for a month again, and in a six-month outpatient program after that.

JUDY K. HERMAN

Was her second episode less severe? What was it like with a new baby?

MARK LUKACH

It was less severe. I remember telling the ER psychiatrist that we had been here, and I knew how to help her. The psychiatrist pulled me out of the room and told me that we hadn't been through this because we didn't have a baby the first time. Having a baby changes everything. She told me I couldn't give my wife the same kind of care because I had a dependent infant who needed my help. She was right.

Giulia stayed in the hospital for a longer time because they wanted her psychosis to resolve before she came home to a baby. Unfortunately, she went through a lengthy depression with suicidal thoughts once she came home.

All three people in the house had very different energies. Taking care of what our six-month-old wanted and needed and taking care of my wife's wants and needs was difficult for me. Her second episode was hardest for me because I had to hold space for two people with very different needs.

JUDY K. HERMAN

Did you have a support system in place then?

MARK LUKACH

Yes. We didn't have family who lived nearby, but I did have a therapist who I started seeing during Giulia's first episode. That was crucial for me. It gave me a place where I could process the grieving I was feeling as well as the fear, anger, and resentment. I wasn't proud to feel that way, but I did.

JUDY K. HERMAN

A few years ago, I had a client who was going through what you went through. And I recommended your book to him. It gave him so much insight and helped his attitude. You can't help but have resentment and anger when going through such traumatic events like this.

MARK LUKACH

Of course, it wasn't her fault, but it did feel like she disrupted our life and the plans we made. She didn't do this by choice. She didn't want this to happen. And yet, irrationally, I wanted to blame someone.

JUDY K. HERMAN

How much insight did Giulia have after her episodes and the effects they had on you and the family?

MARK LUKACH

During the first episode, she had no insight because I hid everything from her. That's when I started writing to make sense of what was happening. It was a form of communication where Giulia could hear what I was saying. She was better. And after I held it together for 10 months, I finally fell apart.

She didn't understand why I wasn't happier once she got better. She wanted to go back to having fun. I had to explain to her that because she was better now, I could show the cracks in my armor that I had been barely holding together for the last ten months.

We were having a difficult time communicating. And I discovered that by writing my feelings I could express myself better. When we speak, our words are a rough draft of our thoughts, and they don't always come out how we want them to. When you write, you get to rephrase and edit your words.

If I wrote something down, I was sure what I was saying was what I intended to say. Then Giulia would read it when she was prepared to read it, instead of it being blurted out at the dinner table. That became really important for us. Because I felt like 99.9% of our life was Giulia's illness and only .1% was me. Relationships can't sustain like that.

I had to make sure she understood my point of view. I would tell her things like, "Yes, it was nice that our parents were offering help, but the help felt oppressive to me. I know I had to make some of these choices, but it was because I was afraid for your life and your safety. You need to understand that's what drove my actions."

She had no awareness of this until I told her.

JUDY K. HERMAN

I learned about anosognosia[9] which is a condition in the brain that makes it impossible for people to have insight to connect the dots from the past to the present. In Dr. Amador's book, *I'm Not Sick and I Don't Need Help*,[10] it's noted that 40% of people who have bipolar disorder and 50% of people with schizophrenia have anosognosia.

I read your book back-to-back with Dr. Amador's book which helped me have compassion for my former husband that I wouldn't have had otherwise.

MARK LUKACH

I don't think Giulia experienced that. I think she was in a state of denial because this happened in her mind. After her first episode she felt shame and was in denial about being sick. During her second episode we had to accept that this was something that wasn't going to go away.

It was going to be part of our lives. We had to make peace with that. We had to plan for the future while knowing how to support her experience of mental illness, and my experience of how her mental illness made me feel.

In a bizarre way the second episode, which was significantly more challenging with the baby, led to more meaningful healing in our relationship with each other. If it had only happened once, we probably would have talked about it to an extent. Then we would have buried it and left it in the past. Because it happened again, we realized we had to look this beast in the face and deal with it.

JUDY K. HERMAN

Did the doctors talk to you about the possibility it was going to happen again?

MARK LUKACH

They did tell us that 90% of people who experience psychosis will experience it again. We knew that. But we kept reverting to the hope we would be part of the 10%. They were always very cautious. And when Giulia got pregnant with our oldest, she had a full medical team to support her with that.

This wasn't willy-nilly. It was very intentional and thought through. She had a lot of check-ins with her psychiatrist at that time.

There was a lot of hope that her episode would be a one-off thing because they called her first episode depression with psychotic features. I interpreted that as a fancy way to say Giulia had a one-off episode that wouldn't happen again. I was wrong. There was no family history, and it didn't come on until later in life. There were a lot of missing puzzle pieces.

During the second episode, it was a different ballgame. This is when the doctors realized they should have kept her on lithium[11] because that was the stabilizing medication, not her antidepressant.

JUDY K. HERMAN
Your wife ended up having a third episode?

MARK LUKACH
She had episodes in 2009, 2012, and 2014. The third episode felt different because we planned for it. After losing the illusion this would never happen again, we realized we had to figure out a way to deal with the logistics if she had another episode.

We had to figure out what would happen with work, our baby, and grandmas whose help I didn't always want. It's complicated because their desire to help comes from a place of love. And they have good intentions. But everyone is processing and interpreting what is going on in their own way. If there are too many cooks in the kitchen it can be challenging to navigate an issue. I don't want to invalidate or discredit the help our families gave to support us. But sometimes, what we needed was space.

After her second episode we talked through many of these issues. This is also when my writing became more public. After the first episode, Giulia and I decided our story could help someone in my position feel less alone and help people in Giulia's position who felt a lot of shame around their mental illness.

It was after the second episode when our message began to feel more valuable. After her first episode, we thought it was a terrible one-off situation. But it was after her second episode we realized crisis and trauma repeats itself. We needed to figure out how to maintain a sense of family while going through crisis and trauma that repeats itself. Once we learned that, we wanted to share that message in the book.

JUDY K. HERMAN
Was the third episode less severe?

MARK LUKACH
It wasn't less severe. We just handled it better. She wasn't any less psychotic. We kept her home longer than the previous two episodes because we thought we could handle it. It was still rough. But she was less afraid of having an episode the third time.

I also had learned how to be her advocate. I learned how to listen to her without making assumptions just because I thought I knew what was best for her. I learned how to let Giulia speak for herself, which was an important lesson.

JUDY K. HERMAN

The love and bond you two have is amazing and touching. In my first book I wrote:

> *"Those who live with a delicacy and the fierceness of mental illness need fortress strength in their partnership with each other. It's absolutely essential to have community support and compliance to treatment. Otherwise, the non-ill spouse's health is at stake."[12]*

I think that describes you and Giulia beautifully. You've learned to be partners.

MARK LUKACH

I couldn't agree with you more. Although I want to put an important caveat to what you're saying. A big fear I had after sharing our story is that we sort of set it up that if you don't stay together you are somehow failing. And I don't agree with that at all.

Despite how hard our circumstances were, we were still really fortunate. We had insurance, so this didn't ruin us financially. Giulia was a compliant patient, which not all patients are. Giulia ultimately found a treatment plan and lifestyle that has helped her stay balanced since 2014.

That doesn't happen for everyone. If we were having this conversation after 12 episodes, this conversation would be much different. Instead, I'm sitting here eight years removed from Giulia's last psychotic episode.

So, I don't believe breaking up is a failure or an abandonment of the sick spouse. The non-ill person needs to take care of themselves, or their health is at stake. It must be taken seriously.

JUDY K. HERMAN

It's remarkable that you wrote this book, and that Giulia gave you the permission to use the title *My Lovely Wife in the Psych Ward*. That took a tremendous amount of character on her part.

MARK LUKACH

I agree. If you Google me, the results show I'm the author and husband who wrote the book and stayed by her side. If you Google her name, she's the psychotic patient. She has shown so much vulnerability and courage by allowing me to share her story. One of the reasons she let me share her story is because she sees that her illness has affected both of us. For her, my experience can speak to the under-explored suffering of caregiving.

When she was going through her recovery, she found recovery role models. They were people who had been sick but found a way to still be successful in their lives, whether that success was in their relationship, career, or a combination of both.

Giulia hopes she can be considered "a success story." She had been hospitalized and felt intense suicidal feelings. And now she's a mother of two, still in a relationship, and still working a high stress job. Hopefully, she can give hope to people.

I've given up on social media, but she's still active on social media and I know it's because she likes to connect with people and help support them through their experiences. Rather than keeping her experience to herself, she wants to share it to help others.

JUDY K. HERMAN

What advice does Giulia share with others who have a mental illness?

MARK LUKACH

The part of her journey she reflects on the most is her path to accepting that she has this condition. It wasn't an easy journey. There was a lot of denial and shame. That has been the single most important place she's gotten to.

She knows she has bipolar disorder but that isn't all she is. That is part of her, and it's not purely negative. It hasn't only brought pain because she's learned so much. People who are facing their own mental health crisis need to make space for it and not let it be the only thing that defines them.

JUDY K. HERMAN

I know you have a deep love for each other. I'm amazed by the bond you two share. How has this defined your marriage? How has this whole process changed you as a husband and a dad?

MARK LUKACH

Writing the book was important for our marriage. Writing became the way we processed what was going on. I would write my experience and Giulia would ask questions and I would answer them. That made us process things together that we might have otherwise avoided doing together. This gave us tremendous empathy for each other. Our capacity to hear each other and make space for each other's experiences was increased tenfold by going through this together.

When we decided to turn this into a book, I would write a chapter in the evening, after school. I would work for a few hours, and it would take me a week or two to write and edit. Then I would send it to Giulia, and she would read through it. Then we would talk about it over the course of a week.

That pattern was therapeutic. When I say therapeutic, I don't mean I felt like I was wrapped in warm blankets and playing with puppies. Therapy is actually ripping your guts out. We had to go through that, and we went through it together. I felt heard and seen in a way that I had never experienced before.

By making the adjustments based on Giulia's input, she felt seen. The ultimate product we ended up putting out is something we're both proud of. It feels very collaborative. It's clear I wrote it, but it's also clear we say, "our book," instead of, "my book."

JUDY K. HERMAN
Are you surprised by the impact of your book?

MARK LUKACH
I am surprised and I'm not. Before releasing the book, I wrote a column in *Modern Love* in the *New York Times*. I received so many emails from people who read my article who told me they felt like someone was finally telling their side of the story. So, I knew there was an audience for my book. I landed Harper Collins, which felt incredible as a high school history teacher. They really pumped up the book and were hopeful. I am perpetually humbled, however, when I hear about people who found my book and needed it.

I think about where the conversation around mental health was in 2009, and where it was when my book was published in 2017. I'm not sure it would have been as well received like it was in 2017. There was a void of perspectives on this topic, which is why our book was received better than I ever could have imagined.

Sometimes I feel weird about its success because I get a lot of emails. And while I feel humbled, I feel responsible to those people. I am bad about engaging with those emails because they are often so heavy and serious. In this process I realized I needed to learn to take care of myself and set my own boundaries.

My heart goes out to people who are going through something similar in their family. As much as I wish I could drive to their house and sit for hours as an empathetic listener, I also have two kids to put to bed and my job to consider. It feels selfish taking care of myself because I do want to help others. But then I recognize that by writing this book, I did help others.

JUDY K. HERMAN
It's never selfish to take care of yourself. You are God's gift to this planet, and nobody can do for you what you can do for yourself. Many caregivers give so much, and that will make them sick if they aren't taking care of themselves.

What advice would you tell your 27-year-old self now?

MARK LUKACH
There are the granular lessons, like learn about mental illness and don't be ignorant about such an important topic. The bigger lesson would be to learn acceptance. People are not who

you think they are or how you manifest them in your fantasies. They are who they are.

As much as I was in love with Giulia, I was also in love with the Giulia I concocted through our interactions. I am proud of myself. I fought for my family, and I gave it my all. Now, I've learned struggle is real, it's okay, and it's no one's fault. You can make it through together. You just have to hang on and be patient.

JUDY K. HERMAN
Did you go to couples therapy through some of this?

MARK LUKACH
I went to a therapist once a week for three years. I realized I reached a point where my entire life couldn't be about caregiving. And we went to group therapy that wasn't great for us because we were having the same fights. We weren't behaving. We were fighting like cats and dogs.

The writing became our therapy because it allowed the tone of the conversation to be different. The book allowed us to understand that yelling at each other doesn't work. We needed to approach each other with some gentleness.

JUDY K. HERMAN
God never wastes any of our pain. There is always a purpose to it.

There was such purpose in this beautiful memoir you wrote. It has touched my heart and the hearts of so many others.

SUMMARY

1. Support and self-care are crucial along with recalibrating expectations when caring for a loved one with mental illness.

2. Writing and helping others can bring healing along with other types of therapeutic support. For spousal partnerships, shared perspectives are necessary to sustain a marital bond.

3. If breaking up is necessary, it's not failure or abandonment of the sick spouse. Rather, the non-ill spouse's health is at stake and must be taken seriously.

JUDY'S CHAPTER TAKEAWAYS

Even though Mark was my guest, in reality, both he and Giulia gave us a remarkable gift of sharing their story.

For those of us who are natural caregivers; my message to you is this. Caring for yourself is NOT selfish. It's vitally important for the "non-ill" spouse to continually focus on self-care, wellness, and self-compassion.

Mark's question is profound. It's necessary to ask, "How do you maintain a sense of family when you know that crisis and trauma might be on a loop cycle?"

Here are some other takeaways in order to have fortress strength in partnership with one who struggles with severe mental illness.

1. Together, embracing and accepting the reality of the illness
2. Compliance to treatment
3. Lifestyle changes, insurance, and a strong support system

To watch this interview, download your free toolkit: go to relationshipswithpurpose.com

Mark Lukach is the author of the international bestselling memoir *My Lovely Wife in The Psych Ward*. His freelance writing has been published in the *New York Times*[13], *The Atlantic*[14], *Pacific Standard*[15], *Wired*[16], and other publications.

He is currently the ninth grade Dean at The Athenian School, where he also teaches history. Mark lives with his wife, Giulia, and their sons in the San Francisco Bay area.

TO CONTACT MARK

✉ mark@marklukach.com

🔗 https://www.marklukach.com/

CHAPTER 5

HOW TO LIVE BETTER,
EVEN WITH DISTRACTIONS

•••••••••

The ADHD Marriage
with Melissa Orlov

JUDY K. HERMAN

I've noticed in my private practice, [1] as I work with entrepreneurial couples and influencers, that some clients experience mood disorders or ADHD. The positive characteristics they have include their creativity and the ability to think bigger. That seems to be a common thread with high-performing clients. Have you seen that kind of correlation?

MELISSA ORLOV

Emotional regulation is a core part of adult ADHD. They may or may not have mood disorders, but certainly there's a lot of emotional dysregulation issues for people impacted by ADHD.

When I see entrepreneurs and work with them, I see a great deal of creativity. If you think of the ADHD brain as one that follows a lot of different paths, that is a positive thing for somebody who's entrepreneurial. You're not afraid to follow a path, see where it goes, get really invested in it, and maybe hyper focus on it for a while.

I see a lot of what is sometimes called impulsivity. You can think of it as impulsivity of thought when it comes to creating new ideas as an entrepreneur. That's a large component to ADHD as well. There are many entrepreneurs who have ADHD.

JUDY K. HERMAN
First of all, would you give a basic definition of ADHD (Attention Deficit Hyperactivity Disorder)[2]?

MELISSA ORLOV
ADHD is about neurochemistry in the brain. Typically, people inherit it. Occasionally people get it from brain trauma. People who have it don't have enough of certain chemicals, particularly dopamine. Dopamine is part of the attention in the reward system.

The number one symptom for people who have ADHD, particularly adults, is being chronically distracted. They are constantly moving their attention from one thing to another.

ADHD is misnamed because it's not attention deficit. Rather, it's attention dysregulation. For example, someone with ADHD might pay a lot of attention to something that's of interest to them. Yet, they have great difficulty focusing on something they're *not* interested in.

People who have ADHD typically are chronically distracted.

Many of them are impulsive and they have very energetic brains with lots of things going on. They often have difficulty either initiating or completing tasks for a variety of reasons.

- Some have short term memory issues.
- Some have coexisting conditions like depression or anxiety.
- There's emotional dysregulation.

The symptoms are all the same, because that's the definition of ADHD. But how it presents in people varies.

JUDY K. HERMAN

ADHD is more about attention dysregulation because of certain deficiencies of neurochemicals in the brain. The number one symptom for adults is distractibility.

How can people move through their lives without knowing they have ADHD until their thirties or forties?

MELISSA ORLOV

They've had ADHD all along, but they've been overcompensating for it. For example, if you're single, it doesn't matter if you complete the tasks because you're totally in charge of everything. Nobody's depending on you to complete most tasks. Even when you are a couple but don't have children, there's a lot of leeway and flexibility in the relationship.

Typically, people start to have more problems when they start to have kids because the uninteresting but necessary tasks multiply like crazy. The expectations about how each person is going to perform and the urgency to perform those tasks also change. This is when people who have less extreme ADHD start experiencing symptoms.

JUDY K. HERMAN

For those who have it, it's common for ADHD to show up later in life because of increased family responsibilities.

MELISSA ORLOV

When they look back at their school records, their childhood, or different choices they made in their careers, they can see it.

ADHD is real and there are studies that back this up and show how much it can impact someone's life. Just because you cope well enough with the symptoms doesn't mean you don't have ADHD or that ADHD isn't real.

JUDY K. HERMAN

I was diagnosed with ADHD later in life. And I was very skeptical of the diagnosis because I didn't think I could have gotten that far in my life without knowing. I didn't understand how I could have received straight A's in my master's degree program and be diagnosed with ADHD.

My psychologist told me I had been overcompensating all this time.

MELISSA ORLOV

Because you've always lived your life that way, you didn't realize how hard you were working to compensate for it. This is exemplified where somebody does very well at school or at work. ADHD doesn't say anything about how smart you are. People who are smart have ADHD. People who are not as smart also have ADHD. It's not correlated to intelligence.

There are people, however, who will say they can't have ADHD because they are successful at work. And they are, because they have a different kind of structure set up and set of goals at work. When they go home, they tend to be more enmeshed in the things that are of less interest to their ADHD brain.

They don't have innate organizational structure unless they create it. These are things people with ADHD struggle with. If someone is really successful, that doesn't mean they can't have ADHD.

JUDY K. HERMAN

Having ADHD has nothing to do with intelligence or success at work. Although the struggle may show up at home.

Can you see differences in the ADHD brain through brain scans?

MELISSA ORLOV

The research suggests the size of different parts of the brain is different for people who have ADHD. And the logical thinking part of the brain matures about three years later. It's not diagnostic to look at a brain scan, even though some folks tell you it is. That's not what the general agreement is in the professional world.

JUDY K. HERMAN

Should people go to a psychologist for testing to get an official diagnosis?

MELISSA ORLOV

A psychologist or a psychiatrist is best. People can go to their family physicians. But they aren't as helpful because they aren't as versed in ADHD and ways to manage it. Treating ADHD isn't only about taking medication. It's about finding things that make your brain function, which includes better sleep, exercise, and medication. Then you must make behavioral changes to help you stay more organized and finish tasks.

People with ADHD must examine how it affects their relationships, how their symptoms are expressed, and how they do or don't follow through on their commitments. Their partner needs to examine how he or she responds to their symptoms. Then they can make a huge shift in how happy they are as a couple if they're aware of all the ways of managing ADHD in their lives.

JUDY K. HERMAN

Treating ADHD is not just about taking medication. Rather, it includes adequate sleep and exercise along with behavioral changes for more structure.

What happens when both spouses have undiagnosed ADHD and they have two or three kids and at least two of those kids also have ADHD? Are those ingredients for messy relationships?

MELISSA ORLOV

Having ADHD in your relationship doesn't guarantee you're going to have troubles. But it does increase the likelihood quite a bit. Often that's because people don't understand ADHD and they don't interpret it correctly.

For example, your partner is chronically distracted from you and not paying very much attention to you. If you don't know about ADHD, you're likely to think your partner has lost interest in you or maybe doesn't love you. Whereas if you *do* know ADHD is there and is real, you can realize your partner still loves you but is distracted right now. Then you can suggest going on a date or doing something to reconnect the two of you.

Those actions have different outcomes. Knowing about ADHD is critical, so people don't make basic ADHD relevant mistakes in their relationship.

JUDY K. HERMAN

There can be better outcomes in a relationship if people understand and interpret ADHD better.

What would you say to the skeptics who think people use ADHD as an excuse to not follow through?

MELISSA ORLOV

I'm empathetic when I hear a spouse tell their partner they are using ADHD as an excuse. For example, maybe they have been talking to their partner about a problem, like not following through with promises. When their partner apologizes for not following through, and then blames it on the ADHD, they might feel as though their partner isn't trying to change. They think their partner is using ADHD as an excuse.

The person who has ADHD is responsible for owning their actions *and* managing their ADHD adequately. No one who has ADHD is going to be cured of it. That's not the way it works. You can learn, however, to have a system in place that makes sure you follow through with your promises or to not promise something you won't follow through with.

JUDY K. HERMAN

The person who has ADHD won't be cured of it. But they can manage it by putting systems in place. They are still responsible for their actions like following through with promises.

MELISSA ORLOV

You can start to work through ADHD and realize it was harder to complete or initiate tasks when it was unmanaged. Then you can start to take those kinds of things into account.

Each partner is responsible for bringing their best self to the relationship. For the ADHD partner, that includes managing the ADHD symptoms. For the non-ADHD partner, that includes learning more about ADHD. It's about being more empathetic towards the difficulties it can present. And it's working with the partner to figure out how to traverse the unexpected ground that's created there.

JUDY K. HERMAN

Yes, the ADHD partner is responsible for managing the symptoms. And the non-ADHD partner is responsible for learning about it and becoming more empathic.

MELISSA ORLOV

It's never a good idea to diagnose your partner. I see this regularly because people are desperate to figure out what is going on. Then they come across information about ADHD and decide that must be it.

If they are on a mission to prove they are right, the person with presumed ADHD feels under attack or blamed. If one partner is blaming the other partner's ADHD for everything wrong in their relationship, that partner isn't taking accountability for the roles they played in the relationship.

I tell people to focus on the actions and the issues instead of the label. Pull in knowledge about ADHD. If someone has it, they are learning about it and can recognize it. If you have ADHD and people show you what ADHD looks like, you're likely going to recognize yourself.

JUDY K. HERMAN

What if a wife has done research and frustration has built up? She wants to help her husband, but he doesn't even go to his regular doctor checkups. What should she do? He's resistant to thinking there is anything he needs to improve. How would you help a couple like that?

MELISSA ORLOV

First, it's good to have a sense of humility. You cannot force somebody to agree with you no matter how strongly you feel you're right. I tell people to back up and try to create a sense of recognition.

In the book *The ADHD Effect on Marriage*[3], there's a chapter that shows the patterns couples commonly fall into like the parent/child dynamic. It's like the symptom response pattern. I suggest picking a few very short paragraphs about specific patterns you recognize in your own relationship. And read them out loud to your partner. Tell your partner you think that sounds like your relationship. And then get a sense of some buy-in through that.

JUDY K. HERMAN

Reading short paragraphs aloud from the chapter about common patterns can invite an open conversation.

MELISSA ORLOV

If the conversation has been going on for a long time, I tell people who can afford it to get an evaluation.[4] One of two things will happen: either you don't have it and you can say to your partner that you do not have ADHD, or you do have it.

If you or your partner does have ADHD, you should be looking into resources that can help you now. Getting an evaluation is a win-win situation. They're not cheap, but they are worth it if your marriage is hanging in the balance.

JUDY K. HERMAN

What would be the course of treatment if someone refuses to take psychotropic medication?

MELISSA ORLOV

20% to 30% of adults with ADHD won't be able to find a medication that works for them without side effects. The good news is, that means 70% to 80% *will* be able to find a medication that works without any significant side effects. And that makes a big difference.

There are different ways to treat ADHD.[5] Each one of these treatments has what is called an effect size. An effect size is a way of measuring the amount of improvement you might, on average, expect to get from a certain kind of treatment.

Medications are used, in part, because they're at the top of that list if you go in descending order. Other things are good as well, two of them being exercise and sleep.

JUDY K. HERMAN
It's important to know that there are other ways to treat ADHD besides medication.

MELISSA ORLOV
A lot of people who have untreated ADHD are athletes. Sports and exercise help them manage their ADHD. Exercise also provides mood stabilization while providing focus.[6] Aerobic exercise provides focus for two to three hours after you do it. So, you can use it tactically, like at lunchtime, if you have afternoons that aren't very productive. You can use exercise to improve your mood management and mood stabilization.

Sleep also helps people with ADHD. Sleep deprivation, even a half hour less than what you're supposed to get, mimics ADHD and being drunk. The measurements are extreme. It's surprising. A lot of people with ADHD have trouble sleeping. People with ADHD must focus on setting a schedule that trains their body to go to bed at a certain time and wake up at a certain time. Many people with ADHD also have sleep disorders, such as sleep apnea. Sleep and exercise are two of the best brain changing things.

JUDY K. HERMAN
To iterate, exercise and sleep are crucial factors in managing ADHD. Sleep deprivation mimics ADHD and being intoxicated!

Can ADHD be treated with mindfulness practices, seeing a coach, or cognitive therapy alone?

MELISSA ORLOV

Mindfulness training helps people slow down or pause, particularly if they have impulsivity.[7] Working with a coach is great for training in executive functioning skills. This includes staying organized, getting things done, or being on time.

There are many ways to manage your ADHD. Medication is faster and very effective relative to the other actions you can take. If people can't take medication that's fine. I remind them that these medications are fast acting and leave our bodies quickly.

If you try a stimulant for one or two weeks, you gain knowledge about how that stimulant can help you. Some people are flabbergasted at the improvement. But they don't have to be committed to taking it long term. People can use a trial to see how it works for them.

JUDY K. HERMAN

I've learned that sleep deprivation is such a baseline for so many mental illnesses. Share more about sleep factors for people with ADHD.

MELISSA ORLOV

Sleep deprivation is included in the symptoms of ADHD. Sometimes people don't have ADHD, but they are sleep deprived. If you do have ADHD, the symptoms become more severe if you don't get enough sleep or if you're under a lot of stress.[8]

JUDY K. HERMAN

Can you speak to how other mental illnesses, like bipolar, can have the same symptoms as ADHD?

MELISSA ORLOV

I'm not a bipolar expert and I'm also not a doctor, so I try not to talk about those too much. They look somewhat similar. You can have them both. But there is a rhythm to the highs and lows of bipolar.[9]

The one thing that I focus on when I talk to people about bipolar versus ADHD is to make sure they understand the medications that are used for ADHD can set off bipolar manic episodes. This is one reason to have a good evaluation. You want to make sure you know what you have so you don't, by mistake, do something to yourself you don't want to do.

JUDY K. HERMAN

It's crucial to know that symptoms of a mood disorder can be similar to ADHD. Also, that a good evaluation is important in order not to set off manic episodes by taking the wrong medication.

Relationships are challenging enough without having to deal with undiagnosed ADHD.

MELISSA ORLOV

The patterns created by a couple where one or both partners have ADHD are predictable. The symptoms are defined, and the responses of the other partner are normal human responses. Distraction is the number one symptom of ADHD. And that distraction translates into neglecting to pay attention to your partner. Then, the human response is to try to get more attention in the relationship. So, they start doing things to get more attention, even yelling.

Once people know what those patterns are, they can interrupt those patterns and change the direction of their relationship.[10]

JUDY K. HERMAN

Knowledge of those predictable patterns is the beginning of changing them.

MELISSA ORLOV

That might sound easy when I say it. But interrupting those patterns includes managing ADHD and managing those responses. Both of those things are a challenge. But I've seen couples take on that challenge and do well.

JUDY K. HERMAN

Many of the lessons in your book are also helpful for people who don't have ADHD. We co-create this dynamic with things we learned in our childhood that we inadvertently take into our adult relationships. They don't work in an adult relationship. However, it's important to raise awareness whether it's self-awareness or relationship awareness. It's equally important to be intentional. Your book can help so many people who recognize themselves with ADHD symptoms.

MELISSA ORLOV

The ADHD Effect on Marriage is my starter book. It gives an overview of ADHD and talks about the path to take to heal your relationship.

My second book, *The Couple's Guide to Thriving with ADHD,*[11] digs deeply into what I call emotional hotspots where couples get stuck. For example, the parent-child dynamic is where one person is the manager, and the other person is the underachiever. There's a lot of friction between the manager and the underachiever as a couple, and my second book delves into that.

JUDY K. HERMAN

Imagine a couple is stuck even though they've seen a therapist and they have ADHD symptoms. What piece of advice would you give them?

MELISSA ORLOV

They should learn as much as they can about ADHD. There are general things that all couples impacted by ADHD need to improve upon. It's important to remember there is this individual aspect to ADHD.[12]

Somebody might have highly emotional ADHD and somebody else might have disorganized ADHD because the relative strength of their symptoms is different. Learning as much as you can and figuring out which tools and which strategies work for you is enlightening and helpful.

JUDY K. HERMAN

Is ADHD more common than people realize?

MELISSA ORLOV

5% to 7% of adults have ADHD, but there's a large group of people who are subclinical. They don't have all the symptoms, but they have some of the symptoms. That number could be as high as 20%. That's a lot of people. So, it's a big deal.

If you're subclinical, either of my books could help you. My work is based not only on ADHD research but also on generalized marital research that works for couples. Then I take those ideas and I adapt them to needs of people with

ADHD. If you only have one or two ADHD symptoms the information in my book is still relevant, even though the proportion of adults with full blown diagnosable ADHD hasn't changed.

SUMMARY

1. ADHD is more about attention dysregulation with distraction being the number one symptom.

2. Knowledge of ADHD and the predictable relationship patterns is the beginning of making positive changes.

3. A correct diagnosis along with coaching or counseling can improve relationships and overall well-being.

JUDY'S CHAPTER
TAKEAWAYS

This conversation with Melissa was so insightful for me both personally and clinically. Her response to my questions about resistance was very gracious and empathic. She brings hope to couples with clinical or subclinical symptoms of ADHD. In my opinion, her books, teachings, and resources are valuable whether or not you or your partner have symptoms or an official diagnosis of ADHD. It's great marriage advice overall.

I resonate with her insights about predictable relationship patterns which I call "relationship dances." You *can* increase your awareness about ADHD, which then gives you the ability to change those patterns. To download your free toolkit including the audio and video versions of this interview, go to relationshipswithpurpose.com

Melissa Orlov is the founder of ADHDmarriage.com, and author of two award-winning books on the impact of ADHD in relationships, *The ADHD Effect on Marriage* and *The Couple's Guide to Thriving with ADHD*. She is considered one of the foremost authorities on the topic of how ADHD impacts adult relationships.

As a marriage consultant, Melissa helps ADHD-affected couples from around the world re-balance their relationships and learn to thrive through her seminars, consulting, and books. She teaches marriage counselors and other professionals about effective marriage therapy for couples impacted by ADHD.

TO CONTACT MELISSA

✉ https://www.adhdmarriage.com/contact

🔗 https://www.adhdmarriage.com/

CHAPTER 6

HOW TO BUILD BETTER AFTER BETRAYAL

· · · · · · · · ·

5 Steps to Transform & Trust Again
with Dr. Debi Silber

JUDY K. HERMAN

Many of my counseling clients and couples come in because they're in pain. They've tried working through betrayal on their own, but then realize they need help. You have a story that fuels your passion to focus on healing from betrayal. May we begin there?

DR. DEBI SILBER

I started in health, then moved to mindset and then to personal development. My family painfully betrayed me. I thought I had done what I needed to do to heal from that. But then it happened again a few years later with my husband.

Anyone who has been betrayed by their husband is shocked, blindsided, devastated, and their lives are no longer the same. I got him out of the house and looked at the two experiences.

I asked myself what, besides me, was common between these two betrayals. That's when I realized my boundaries were always being crossed and I never took my needs seriously.

I believe that if nothing changes, nothing changes. I had four kids, six dogs, a thriving business and I decided to go back to get my PhD. I didn't know how I was going to pay for it or how I was going to manage it. It was something, however, I knew I needed to do.

I entered the program. And when it was time to do a study, I decided to study betrayal. I studied what holds us back and what helps us heal. I studied what happens to people, physically, mentally, and emotionally when the people closest to us lie, cheat, or are deceitful. That study led to three groundbreaking discoveries, which changed my health, my business, my family, and my life.

JUDY K. HERMAN
Share more about those groundbreaking discoveries.

DR. DEBI SILBER
Originally, I was studying betrayal and post-traumatic growth[1]. Post-traumatic growth is how the crisis you went through, whether it was the death of a loved one, disease, or a natural disaster, leaves you with new awareness, insight, and perspective you didn't have before.

For example, maybe you lose someone, and you realize how short life is and how it shouldn't be taken for granted. I had experienced the death of a loved one, and disease too. And I thought that betrayal felt different. I didn't assume it was the same for all the participants in the study. So, I asked them if they felt the same way. And unanimously they said they did.

Then they explained why betrayal felt different. Betrayal feels intentional, so we take it personally. They felt rejection and abandonment. Their entire selves felt shattered including belonging, confidence, worthiness, and trust.

This type of healing needed its own name, which is now called Post Betrayal Transformation (PBT)[2]. Not only are people rebuilding their lives, they're rebuilding themselves. PBT is a complete and total rebuild of someone's life after an experience with betrayal. My first discovery was that betrayal felt different from other crises.

JUDY K. HERMAN

Betrayal *does* feel different from other types of crises. What are the differences between betrayal and PTSD (Post-Traumatic Stress Disorder)[3]?

DR. DEBI SILBER

PTSD symptoms are very common in a betrayal experience. We think PTSD is reserved for the war veteran. They hear a car backfire and they're reminded of that time in war. But that's not always the case.

Someone who's been betrayed can be triggered. A trigger can happen. And their body will react and respond as if it's discovery day, all over again. PBT is rebuilding after that happens. PTSD symptoms are very common when you've been betrayed.

Betrayal lends itself to creating an entirely new identity. You take the parts about you that you love and leave behind what no longer serves you. You can create a version of yourself that never would have shown up without having that experience. That's why PBT is trauma well served.

As I've mentioned, the experience of betrayal is different from other crises because of how *intentional* it feels. For example, if you lose someone you love, you grieve, you're sad, and you mourn the loss. But you don't necessarily think you're crazy. You don't lose trust in everyone around you. You don't take that personally. Betrayal feels very intentional.

JUDY K. HERMAN

Betrayal *feels* very intentional. Yet, this jolting experience lends itself to creating an entirely new identity. I'm curious about the second discovery.

DR. DEBI SILBER

The second discovery was this. There's a collection of symptoms (physical, mental, and emotional) so common in betrayal that there is now Post Betrayal Syndrome. About 60,000 people took our post betrayal syndrome quiz on our website to see how much they were struggling with betrayal.

Many of us have been taught that time heals all wounds. I have proof, when it comes to betrayal, that is not true. At the end of the quiz, we ask participants if there is anything else they would like to share.

We received messages that said, "My betrayal happened 35 years ago. I'm unwilling to trust again." "My betrayal happened 15 years ago. I feel gutted." Because of this, we know that time does not heal all wounds. We can spot an unhealed betrayal a mile away.

JUDY K. HERMAN

So, the first discovery is that betrayal feels intentional which is different than other types of traumatic experiences. The second discovery is that you can identify unhealed betrayal because of common symptoms.

Why do people believe that time heals all wounds?

DR. DEBI SILBER

Time *can* soften the blow. But until we learn the profound lessons in betrayal, we will keep giving people opportunities to betray us. I'm not suggesting that betrayal is our fault. But if we don't learn from it, the opportunity for people to take advantage of us is still there.

JUDY K. HERMAN

Even though time has passed, we need to learn the profound lessons from our experiences of betrayal. Otherwise, we'll inadvertently pave the way for a pattern of betrayal.

DR. DEBI SILBER

For me, my boundaries kept being crossed. I never took my needs seriously. After I experienced my second betrayal, I knew I had enough. Enrolling in that PhD program was the first thing I'd ever done for myself. It was huge. It changed my life. That's the idea. Time doesn't heal betrayal. There are some symptoms that linger, which brings me to my third discovery. Of those 60,000 people, including men, women, every age group, and just about every country:

- 78% constantly revisit their experience
- 81% feel a loss of personal power
- 80% are hyper vigilant
- 94% deal with painful triggers

The most common physical symptoms among those who took the quiz show us that:

- 71% have low energy
- 68% have sleep issues
- 63% have extreme fatigue

They wake up, they are exhausted, and their adrenals have tanked. 47% of people who take the quiz experience weight changes. In the beginning they couldn't hold food down and later they use food for comfort.

45% have a digestive issue, ranging from Crohn's Disease, IBS, diverticulitis, constipation, or diarrhea.

The most common mental symptoms among those who took the quiz demonstrate that:

- 78% are overwhelmed
- 70% are walking around in a state of disbelief
- 68% are unable to focus
- 64% are in shock
- 62% can't concentrate

Imagine having to show up to work every day when you can't concentrate, you're exhausted, and you have a gut issue. If they have kids, they still must raise them too.

Those statistics don't even cover the emotional issues. We found that of the people who took the quiz:

- 88% experience extreme sadness
- 83% are very angry and bounce back and forth between those two emotions
- 82% feel hurt
- 80% have anxiety
- 79% are stressed
- 84% lose the ability to trust
- 67% prevent themselves from forming deep relationships
- 82% find it hard to move forward
- 90% want to move forward but don't know how

That is why I wrote the book, *Trust Again*[4].

This is research we've done since the study. And all those percentages were high. They weren't results with only 20% or 30%. The wildest thing to me about this, however, is that these high percentages can come from betrayals that happened decades ago. People spend decades with gut issues, anxiety, weight issues, and an inability to trust, all from something that happened long ago.

JUDY K. HERMAN
The average mental health or health practitioner isn't aware of these statistics.

DR. DEBI SILBER
That's why we created our certification program. Even if you go to the most well-meaning gut doctor, if he isn't highly skilled in betrayal, he can only take the patient so far. When

people understand what betrayal does, the transformation they have with their patients and clients can be much deeper.

The most exciting of the three discoveries is that people can be stuck for years or decades. But if they're going to fully heal and move from Post Betrayal Syndrome to Post Betrayal Transformation, they're going to go through five proven and predictable stages. We know what happens physically, mentally, and emotionally at each of those stages. We know what it takes to move from one stage to the next.

JUDY K. HERMAN

Again, those three groundbreaking discoveries are:

1. Healing from betrayal is very different than healing from other life crises.
2. There are 5 proven and predictable stages from betrayal to breakthrough.
3. There are identifiable post-betrayal symptoms.

This is giving us hope toward healing if it's predictable. Is experiencing betrayal universal?

DR. DEBI SILBER

It's very unlikely someone *hasn't* experienced betrayal. It could be your best friend shared your secret, your coworker took credit for your idea, as a child your parent did something awful, or someone in a position of authority took advantage of you. There are many faces and phases to betrayal.

JUDY K. HERMAN

Please share about those five stages.

DR. DEBI SILBER

The five stages are as follows. In *stage one*, imagine a table with four legs. And those four legs represent our physical, mental, emotional, and spiritual sides. Everybody, including myself, leaned heavily on their physical and mental sides while not prioritizing their emotional and spiritual sides. Because of this, now the table has two legs. And it's easy for the table to topple over.

Stage two is by far the scariest of all the stages. This stage includes the shock and the trauma experienced on discovery day. It breaks down your body, your mind, and your worldview. You've ignited the stress response. And you're going to have every stress related symptom, illness, condition, or disease.

During this time, your mind is in a complete and total state of chaos and you are totally overwhelmed. You can't wrap your mind around what you just learned. It makes no sense, and your world view has been shattered.

Your worldview is your mental model. It creates the rules that prevent chaos and govern you. In one moment or a series of moments, everything you've known is no longer the same. Every rule has changed. The bottom has bottomed out and a new bottom hasn't been formed. It's terrifying. If you lose your foundation, you hold on to whatever you can to stay safe and alive.

This brings us to *stage three*, which is the most practical of all the stages. This is when people start thinking about how to survive this experience. They are trying to figure out where to go, who they can trust, and how they can feed their kids. This can be a trap though, and this stage is where most people get stuck.

JUDY K. HERMAN

Stage one is realizing the imbalance with our physical, mental, emotional and spiritual sides of ourselves. *Stage two* is the scariest which includes the instability of shock, trauma and overwhelm. *Stage three* is the most practical because you're figuring out logistics. Yet it's the place where most people get stuck.

DR. DEBI SILBER

Once you've figured out how to survive your experience, you think you're good. You don't start transformation until stage four. But because you don't know there's anywhere else to go, you start planting roots in stage three. You're not supposed to, but you don't know that.

Then you start getting small self-benefits. You get to be right. You get your story and you get sympathy from everybody you tell your story to. You have a target for your anger.

If you're receiving any of those benefits, you don't have to do the hard work of learning to trust again. You don't have to think about if you should trust someone or if you can trust someone. You can decide to trust nobody because it's easier that way.

Because you stay in this stage longer than you should, your brain tricks you into thinking maybe you're not that great. Or maybe you deserve what happened to you. So, you plant deeper roots because you don't know you're not supposed to.

JUDY K. HERMAN

The reason most people get stuck in stage three is because they are past the painful part. They do what's easier and are unaware of a better life.

DR. DEBI SILBER

Because this is how you feel and this is the energy around you, that energy attracts like energy. So, now you're inviting situations, circumstances, and relationships that confirm this is where you belong. You're now part of the misery loves company crowd.

It gets worse, but you'll make it out of here. Because it feels so bad and you don't know there is anywhere else to go. You resign yourself. You know you don't like the position you're in, but you think you must find a way to be okay with it.

This is when people start using food, drugs, alcohol, work, and TV to numb, avoid, and distract themselves from facing or feeling pain. After doing it for a day, a week, a month, a year, it becomes a habit.

JUDY K. HERMAN

Being stuck in stage three lends itself to resignation, distraction, avoidance and numbing one's life. Does it become ingrained in their character?

DR. DEBI SILBER

I can see someone who was betrayed 20 years ago, and they are still emotionally eating, drinking, or numbing themselves in front of the TV. If I ask them if they think that has anything to do with their betrayal, they look at me like I'm crazy. They put themselves in stage three and stayed there.

JUDY K. HERMAN

Moving beyond stage three is an opportunity to figure out the lesson and move into transformation in order to live a purposeful life. I'm wondering about the influence of family patterns from previous generations showing stage three living as normal.

DR. DEBI SILBER

That's what they know. It's not that it's good. It's that it's the familiar choice. That's why people get into toxic relationships or go from one abusive relationship to the next. It's something they know how to do. That's the energy of stage three.

You think you're surviving and it's as good as it gets. I wrote the book *Hardened to Healed*[5] to focus only on stage three because I realized how many people were stuck there.

I was looking at the statistics and wondering why people were staying in stage three, when the hardest parts were over. I wanted to understand why people stayed in survival mode instead of embracing the transformation waiting inside them. The seed of transformation is planted through that experience. If you're willing to grieve and mourn that loss, you can move on to stage four.

Stage four is when you find and begin to adjust to your new normal. This is where you acknowledge you can't undo your experience, but you can control what you do with it. By making that mental decision, you turn down your stress response. You're not healing yet, but you stopped the massive damage that was created in stages two and three.

Moving into stage four is like moving into a new house, condo, or apartment. You don't have all your stuff yet, and it's not quite a cozy place. But you have a sense you'll be okay. It's new unfamiliar energy, but you realize this could be a good thing.

JUDY K. HERMAN

I like the analogy of stage four being like moving into a new place that's not quite cozy yet.

DR. DEBI SILBER

Stage four is interesting because you don't take with you the things you don't want to represent you to that new space. If your friends haven't been there for you during this process, this is the stage where you outgrow them. You don't take those people with you from stage three to stage four.

You might be confused by this, but you're undergoing a transformation. And if they don't come with you, you're going to leave them behind. You don't have the headspace for them anymore. You're more discerning about what you want included in this new lifestyle you're creating.

Once you feel comfortable in this space, make it cozy, and mentally make it your home, you move into the *fifth and most beautiful stage*. This is where you experience healing, rebirth, and a new world view. The body starts to heal. You start practicing self-love, self-care, eating well, exercising, and other healthy habits you didn't have the bandwidth for earlier because you were surviving.

Your mind is healing. You're making new rules and new boundaries based on the road you just traveled. You have a new worldview based on everything you see so clearly now.

In the beginning you relied on the mental and physical legs. By this point, you're grounded because you're focused on the emotional and spiritual part of your life too.

JUDY K. HERMAN

Stage five is when you establish comfort in your new world view. You changed your old thinking patterns, friendships, and now have the bandwidth for self-care.

It seems that the fourth stage is the willingness to grieve and grieve thoroughly.

DR. DEBI SILBER

That's a part of stage four. You're changing everything here and that's why it's easy to see the shift from stage three to stage four. This is where you outgrow your friendships because you're changing so much.

This is the caterpillar going into the cocoon and coming out the butterfly. That caterpillar is willing to be emulsified, deconstructed, and unrecognizable from anything it once was. Only because it went through that process does it get to be the butterfly. I'm not going to lie and say it's an easy, simple process because it's not. It is, however, the most transformative thing you'll ever do.

JUDY K. HERMAN

Even though it's not easy or simple, once you're on the other side, the transformation is so worth it! Do people cycle through these phases of betrayal throughout their lives?

DR. DEBI SILBER

The order doesn't change, and you never skip any stages. You move through them. It's not simple and linear. You move forward, but you're going to move back a little before you move forward again. Then you outgrow one stage as you grow into the next.

If you do the work and really make it to stage five, you don't attract the people whom you would have attracted before you did the work. When you are in stage five, you resonate at a different level. You don't attract the kind of person who will betray you.

Most people after they've been betrayed, are devastated, heartbroken, and sad. They want that feeling to go away. So they want that person back or someone new, right then. That is the absolute worst thing to do.

If this person who's been betrayed is committed to the betrayer, they start doing the work, but they keep sabotaging themselves because they don't want to outgrow the person who betrayed them. They get frustrated because they don't understand why they are so committed to being there. But it's because they aren't ready to change.

JUDY K. HERMAN

I can see how it could be a "conflict of interest" when the commitment to the betrayer is greater than their commitment to their personal transformation. They fear outgrowing their partner which may indicate they are not ready for change.

DR. DEBI SILBER

Their job is to be so committed to healing that they either both go their separate ways, or the other person decides to step up and meet the strength of the betrayed person.

Rebuilding is always a choice. You can rebuild yourself and move on. Or, if the situation lends itself and you're willing, you can rebuild something new from the ground up; new with the person who hurt you. That's what I did with my husband. After we became a new couple, we married each other again.

JUDY K. HERMAN

How did you end up remarrying the person who betrayed you?

DR. DEBI SILBER

I'm a highly sensitive empath. Integrity is my highest value. For me, betrayal is one of the worst things a person can do. It was devastating when it happened to me. That was the deal breaker. That was it. That's why he was out the house, and I was figuring out how to be a single mom to four, with six dogs, a business, while starting a PhD program. I had to figure out how to get it together.

At first, I focused on getting through each day. Then I had a moment of clarity, which inspired this study. I was my own case study because I was incorporating everything I learned into my healing journey. One day I realized that if I could heal, I was going to take everybody with me.

JUDY K. HERMAN

Deciding to heal yourself is a gift. How can you take others with you?

DR. DEBI SILBER

I had every reason to stay stuck. All the important people in my life all betrayed me. I had a very powerful story and when I told it to anybody, I got lots of sympathy. But then I realized that was all I would ever get. I realized I could stay sick, sad, and stuck and be the poster child for betrayal. Or I could do something with this and help a lot of people. That was my motivation. My kids were watching me. My husband was the one who told them about the betrayal. I think he transformed in part because he wanted to not only make it up to me but make it up to them as well.

JUDY K. HERMAN

How old were your children when he chose to tell them?

DR. DEBI SILBER

They were teenagers. Betrayal will show you who someone truly is and has the potential to wake them up to see who they temporarily became. You never know what you're going to see, and even if they do wake up, you still don't have to be interested in reconciliation or rebuilding. That wasn't my intention. My intention was to heal and that would be the end of it.

When someone takes their transformation so seriously, there is an opportunity and potential for change there. People are afraid of the complete and utter destruction or death of the old. But that's the only way you can birth the new.

JUDY K. HERMAN

That's a profound concept in transformation. The utter destruction or death of the old in order to birth the new. How did you reunite after all this?

DR. DEBI SILBER

We got married again with new rings, vows, a new dress, and our four children as our wedding party.

JUDY K. HERMAN

Did you go through couple's counseling together?

DR. DEBI SILBER

No. I did the work on my own, and he did the work on his own. And we came back together as totally transformed people.

If a counselor isn't skilled in moving someone through betrayal, it can do more harm than good. Many people come into the PBT Institute with therapy trauma. It's a real thing. If you aren't receiving the right kind of support and don't want to outgrow your group, you can sabotage your own healing. The right type of support makes or breaks it.

JUDY K. HERMAN

What other advice you would like to share?

DR. DEBI SILBER

I know the feeling of betrayal. It's a pain like no other. One of my study participants said that betrayal feels like every negative emotion you can imagine punched in your gut and losing a child in a crowd at the same time. It's awful. I didn't do anything other people can't do. That feeling was so bad that I was determined to find a way through it and create a roadmap for others.

SUMMARY

1. The experience of betrayal is different than other traumas. Because it feels intentional, common symptoms are termed as Post Betrayal Syndrome.

2. There are five stages to healing from betrayal with most people not getting past the third stage.

3. Post Betrayal Transformation (PBT) lends itself to creating an entirely new identity.

JUDY'S CHAPTER TAKEAWAYS

What I love about being in the field of mental health and relationships are encountering my colleagues who are doing such profound work. Dr. Debi Silber is one I deeply admire and whose message resonates with mine.

Her valid research leading to groundbreaking discoveries have heightened my awareness over the effects unhealed betrayal. To identify five predictable stages to PBT (Post Betrayal Transformation) is brilliant. To understand the differences between healing and transformation is gold. It makes so much sense that most people only get to stage three. But stages four and five are pathways that lead to a new and vibrantly authentic life.

In my opinion, there's no better analogy of transformation than the caterpillar turning into a butterfly. Dr. Silber said, it "is willing to be emulsified, deconstructed, and unrecognizable from anything it once was." Natalie Hoffman uses this same illustration. Other guests in this book have described transformation. I'm convinced that's why God made caterpillars and butterflies.

To access your free toolkit along with the video & audio version of this interview: go to relationshipswithpurpose.com

 **Dr. Debi Silber** is the founder of the Post Betrayal Transformation Institute. She is a holistic psychologist and a health, mindset, and personal development expert, along with an award-winning speaker and coach who helps people move past their betrayals. Dr. Silber's recent PhD study on how we experience betrayal made 3 groundbreaking discoveries that showed how long it takes to heal.

She is the author of *Trust Again*[6]. She is also a two-time #1 International bestselling author of: T*he Unshakable Woman*[7] AND *From Hardened to Healed: The Effortless Path to Release Resistance, Get Unstuck, and Create a Life You Love.* Her podcast: *From Betrayal to Breakthrough*[8] is also globally ranked within the top 1.5% of podcasts.

TO CONTACT DR. SILBER

✉ ClientCare@PBTInstitue.com

🔗 https://thepbtinstitute.com/

CHAPTER 7

HOW TO HEAL BETTER BEYOND ADDICTIONS

·········

Going Deeper
with Dr. Eddie Capparucci

JUDY K. HERMAN

Share about your work as a couple helping individuals and other couples in the area of addictions.

DR. EDDIE CAPPARUCCI

I got involved in the ministry as a licensed therapist who specializes in sex and porn addiction. My wife Terry works with the women who have been betrayed by men who are addicted to porn and sex. Together we are trying to help build up individuals by exposing the pain they've gone through. Then we bring them together to reconcile in a way they've never reconciled before because they aren't going to go back to their previous relationship. They must go somewhere new.

That's what our ministry is about. It's wonderful to work with my partner where we see so much healing. We know we are helping people and giving back based on what we've been through ourselves.

JUDY K. HERMAN

How did you and Terry develop to this point of helping others together? In particular, what was your journey of becoming a licensed therapist who specializes in sex and porn addiction?

DR. EDDIE CAPPARUCCI

Terry and I have been married 25 years. She is my third wife. I was actively addicted to porn and sex during my first two marriages. I was a marketing and advertising executive for 25 years. I worked my way up in corporate America and was very successful in what I did. From a relationship standpoint, I was a disaster.

After the second marriage ended, I went and sought help about what was going on. Through that I came to understand I had an attachment disorder. It was an avoidant attachment, and I had no idea what that was about. I just knew that in every relationship since I was 16, I had one foot in and one foot out. This is because my father died when I was five and my mother had a nervous breakdown. As a young child I was sent to live with a relative I didn't know for a year.

I didn't understand why this was happening. No one told me what was going on. They just told me my mom was sick. Later, my two older sisters had to watch over me because mom had to work. They didn't want to watch a six-year-old boy. Instead, they would watch TV and tell me to go to my room.

I was very isolated and alone for the first ten years of my life. I didn't have my first friend until I was almost 10. I created a worldview that said the people I loved will leave me and the people who loved me will disappoint me.

JUDY K. HERMAN

Your vulnerability here gives hope to folks who have had similar experiences.

DR. EDDIE CAPPARUCCI

I don't believe we go from one path to another path. I believe we are haunted by past experiences. How much we are haunted depends on the amount of work we have done. Those wounds produce scars and those scars never fully heal.

In my first book, *Going Deeper: How the Inner Child Impacts Your Addiction*[1], I talk about the unresolved childhood pain point. Events can happen to us today that match up with those past events. That intensifies the level of discomfort we feel. Therefore, it causes us to want to run away from those emotions. And we run away by using bad behavior. Sometimes we may get aggressive and angry. We may withdraw, or worse yet, we wind up acting out in a way that is unhealthy.

JUDY K. HERMAN

Some of our current events match up with familiar past events. This actually reveals unresolved childhood pain points getting our attention in order to heal. Yet, the tendency is to avoid that pain.

DR. EDDIE CAPPARUCCI

I'm a big "why" guy. As therapists, we're trained not to ask the "why" question because it comes across as an accusation. I break that mold. I want to know why I feel and think the way

I do. If we know the answer to those questions, we are empowered to make real changes.

Too many of us are walking around oblivious. We're doing the same thing over and over or thinking or feeling the same way. It's driving us crazy. It's driving our spouses crazy. The problem is, we don't know why we act this way.

JUDY K. HERMAN

Your "why" comes across as curiosity. Some people use their "why" to put the other person on the defensive or to set them up, so they can tear down their argument. I think your "why" is one to foster curiosity.

With your point, our journey in life is to become aware. Life gives us these experiences based upon unconscious or unaware choices. I think that's what your work on the inner child is all about.

DR. EDDIE CAPPARUCCI

I created the inner child model[2] to help with the treatment of addictions. This centers on three different components. It's trauma based and looks at the unresolved childhood pain points. Then it focuses on our ability to sit with emotional distress.

When we can't sit with emotional discomfort, we develop coping mechanisms to deal with it. We are still young and think with an emotional brain instead of a cognitive brain. We try to fix these issues by not thinking about them. Then we find a behavior to distract ourselves and remain in the fantasy we created. Examples include eating too much, watching too much TV, or playing too many videogames.

We take those same coping mechanisms into our teen years and adult years. When continuing to those same behaviors repeatedly, you wind up with addictive behavior. There are so many people who come home and throw themselves in front of the TV until they fall asleep. Then they go back to work and do it again. There is loss of emotional connection that comes from these types of additive behaviors.

JUDY K. HERMAN
Those same coping mechanisms from childhood don't work in adulthood.

I am all about giving people grace because it takes a lot of courage to come to counseling and become aware of destructive and repetitive thoughts and behaviors. Coming to this realization is a starting point. As a child, you *are* a victim of your circumstances. You *are* dependent upon the adults around you and their decisions.

We likely needed those behaviors in order to *survive* our childhoods. It's part of our humanity to move toward pleasure and away from pain. Yet we are designed to grow and become more aware. Our lives and relationships are so valuable.

DR. EDDIE CAPPARUCCI
I tell most of the men I work with they are emotionally immature.

JUDY K. HERMAN
That's a bold statement to say to men. How do they take it?

DR. EDDIE CAPPARUCCI
No one has ever challenged me. They tell me I'm right.

JUDY K. HERMAN

You're a male therapist working with males. Do you think this is information men could receive from a female?

DR. EDDIE CAPPARUCCI

It would be quite difficult for men to have these discussions with women. If the man is open minded and they're looking for self-reflection and a deep understanding of who they are, it shouldn't matter who the information comes from. But it can be more challenging for men to hear these things from a female therapist. The fact of the matter is there are 30- and 40-year-old men who still act like they are 15.

JUDY K. HERMAN

Sometimes men who are dealing with sexual addiction or addiction to pornography will seek out a female therapist. I think it's valuable for men to seek out male therapists in these situations to get some straight talk and have relatability between them. If men are struggling with this, I think it helps to find a male who specializes in this field.

DR. EDDIE CAPPARUCCI

I agree. There are many women who specialize in sex and pornography addiction, but they are dealing with a man who is struggling in a relationship with a woman. He's objectifying women. So, working with a female might be counterintuitive.

JUDY K. HERMAN

When a man struggles with pornography or sex addiction, there is usually a woman on the other side of that relationship. Share more about how your wife, Terry and you work together.

DR. EDDIE CAPPARUCCI

Before Terry came into the practice, I was dealing with the women who were struggling with betrayal. I've seen a lot of that up close and personal. Over the years we've come to understand that when a man has had one or multiple affairs or seeks out sex workers, the wife acts so devastated that people call her a co-addict. Or they say she is codependent. She is blamed for part of his addiction.

Many women who have gone to their clergy for advice have been told they need to be more sexual with their husband. They might be told to wear new lingerie or that they should spice up their relationship. That just retraumatizes them.

Because of the work of Barbara Steffens[3] and other pioneers in this area, we now understand that these women are going through betrayal, which is traumatic. It's like suffering from Post-Traumatic Stress Disorder.[4] So, we must treat it that way and understand what is happening. The counselor needs to be compassionate and understanding. Each person needs to do their own individual work. It's easier to deal with men and their addictive behaviors than it is to deal with their wives who are grieving.

JUDY K. HERMAN

To be identified as a "co-addict" doesn't help a wife who's been betrayed. It's even more traumatizing for her to be advised to "spice up the relationship." No wonder she's devastated and angry.

DR. EDDIE CAPPARUCCI

Most men will die on that hill because hostility is being thrown at them, and rightfully so. Instead of seeing the hostility the men need to see their wives' pain. They need to realize this is pain they have caused and ask how they can help their wife. Instead, they get defensive and try to explain things. They take a bad situation and make it worse.

Terry works with the women and helps them grieve. It's important to remember that women, just like men, have trauma from their pasts too. If their traumas from the past include betrayal, the two worlds merge. It intensifies the level of pain the women are going through. Terry helps them pull their world apart and see what their husband did through a different lens. That takes work. It takes anywhere from 18 months to five years for a woman to recover from the trauma of betrayal.

JUDY K. HERMAN

You are a team with this very delicate and intense work. It's valuable to know the framework and timeline. It takes anywhere from 18 months to five years for a woman to recover from betrayal. That's significant.

The re-traumatization is a lot to unravel, especially coming from a trusted pastor or clergy.

DR. EDDIE CAPPARUCCI

There are some good pastors and clergy members who do understand and don't give that kind of advice. They may get the same advice if they go to a therapist who doesn't specialize in this area.

JUDY K. HERMAN

Yes, it's crucial for a therapist or spiritual leader to be specialized in this area. And there are some who've not gone through their own healing and may also be addicted to porn.

DR. EDDIE CAPPARUCCI

I've worked with clergy. I've worked with athletes. I've worked with television personalities. I've worked with people in government. This is not something that discriminates. Any person can have this disorder because it's not about sex. It's an intimacy disorder based on their unresolved childhood pain points, which we all have to some extent.

JUDY K. HERMAN

Talk about the catalysts that bring men to ask for your help. I wonder if it's the internal moral conflict they feel. Or is it circumstances that bring them to counseling?

DR. EDDIE CAPPARUCCI

It's rare for a man to walk into my office on his own and say he wants help because he's struggling in this area. Usually, something has happened. There's a serious consequence. He's been discovered and his world blew up. He comes in to save his marriage.

I tell them they can't be here to save their marriage. They need to come because they want to change themselves. Everything I do with the inner child model is about self-reflection. It's about learning why they feel and act the way they do.

That won't save their marriage, but it will transform their heart and that's what we're looking to do. We want to create a new guy. The wife doesn't want the old guy anymore. She wants a new guy.

JUDY K. HERMAN

Pain motivates people to come to counseling in the first place. What's the likelihood of a man continuing his inner child work if he discovers his marriage can't be saved? When does he realize the work will benefit him as a human being?

DR. EDDIE CAPPARUCCI

It happens when they get into therapy, see the results, and understand why they act the way they do. They realize they aren't just a pervert or a sleaze ball. There is a reason and rationale to their destructive behavior. Once they see that, they want to learn more because they don't want to go through the same thing again.

After my second marriage, I realized I couldn't live like that anymore and I looked for help. Both of my first two wives wanted to work it out, but I didn't think I could because I thought there was something wrong with me. I thought I was sick. I thought I would still hurt them, and I didn't want to do that anymore. So, I walked away from both.

After walking away from my second marriage, I realized I couldn't live like this anymore and that I needed help. So, I went and did the work and got help. Shortly after that I met Terry. She got the new version of me. Now, we've been married for 25 years, and I've been faithful the whole time.

JUDY K. HERMAN

Would you share how a romantic relationship develops when there are issues of addiction?

DR. EDDIE CAPPARUCCI

When a man who is emotionally undeveloped woos a young

woman, he gets away with it because of hormones generated in the early stages of the relationship. Oxytocin is flowing strongly in the brain, and he feels like this is the most incredible thing he has ever experienced.

He gets married or they stay together a few years, and those hormones start to die down. The neurochemicals return to normal levels and now he's back to where he was.

> He's hypersensitive to criticism.
> He struggles to connect.
> He's inwardly focused.
> He's not content with life.
> He can't sit with his emotional pain.
> He's not mindful.
> He has limited interest and passion.

So, the woman feels like she doesn't know her partner anymore. When this happens, I tell women to find someone who has known her partner for a long time. Tell them what she sees. And I guarantee they're going to say that's him.

Those relationships are rarely built on true emotional connection and intimacy. These guys are emotionally undeveloped and the foundation for their relationships is physical intimacy. They feel most loved when women are physical with them. This is how they receive and express love. Every now and then they sprinkle in some emotional intimacy by buying them flowers or complimenting their hair. But it's very shallow and not ongoing.

JUDY K. HERMAN
You mention the concept of alexithymia in your book. Would

you describe alexithymia and how it affects men who are struggling?

DR. EDDIE CAPPARUCCI

Alexithymia is the inability to emotionally engage or connect. People who suffer from this are going to have a hard time identifying how they feel. This goes back to early childhood development when we didn't learn how to regulate our emotions.

If this teaching is missing, we don't have the words to help us describe our emotions. Therefore, we stay with the emotions of anger, fear, sadness, and happiness. So, when we are upset with something, we may pout or act angry because we don't know how to express how we feel. We don't have the right language to describe our feelings.

JUDY K. HERMAN

They don't have the language to describe their feelings or the meanings behind them. And they aren't aware of where those feelings are showing up in the body. For example, they likely won't say that their heart is racing because they are scared to lose their partner.

DR. EDDIE CAPPARUCCI

Many men feel they can't say something like that because it would be too vulnerable. Even if they can identify what those emotions are, they've been taught that sharing their emotions is dangerous.

JUDY K. HERMAN

Both society and culture have groomed boys and men that way.

DR. EDDIE CAPPARUCCI

Therefore, I can't share my feelings. Because if I do, I'm a wimp. I'm going to look weak. People won't respect me.

Then, if someone wants to share their emotions with them, they become overwhelmed because they don't know what to do with the other person's emotions.

Men don't want to fix problems because they want women to see how brilliant men are. Men fix problems because they want those emotions to go away.

JUDY K. HERMAN

If men can't handle their own emotions, they won't be able to understand the emotions of their wives.

DR. EDDIE CAPPARUCCI

They won't be able to understand their wives, or they will minimize their wives' feelings. They'll tell their wives not to worry about it, that it's not a big deal, it's fine, or that it will work itself out. Ultimately, the men are going to withdraw. They'll say things like, "I don't have time for this," or "I can't deal with this." None of these actions are good for a relationship.

JUDY K. HERMAN

Men don't realize that paradoxically, leaning in to their wives' negative emotions helps them feel connected.

DR. EDDIE CAPPARUCCI

They weren't taught that kind of model. They may have had a parent who smothered them with emotions. For example, I have a client who came to understand that when his father got angry it was his job to make his father happy. He would tell me he had to figure out a way to make his dad calm down.

In cases like this, people give up their autonomy to please their dad. In other cases, they might not have seen a good model of people being emotional. Or they weren't taught emotional regulation. So, they end up with emotions that they don't know how to regulate. They don't know where to put these emotions, so instead they try not to feel them.

JUDY K. HERMAN

Fear is a powerful emotion. The body is unaware of the difference between perceived and real fear. Many of my clients are fearful that they won't be able to move through the emotions. But I assure them that our emotions are temporary. They are like temporary messengers to our souls.

For example, if anxiety, depression, or anger shows up, listen to their messages. Make changes. God created humans to have emotions. Don't detach from them. Rather, embrace them. Listen to them. And then, let them go.

DR. EDDIE CAPPARUCCI

If you detach from your negative emotions, you're going to detach from positive emotions too. Then, you miss out on so much life has to offer. You miss out on what a relationship can offer you. You miss out on a lot of the things that can bring you a sense of joy and peace because you're walking around with a void.

When I worked in corporate America I would say "I'm a successful guy," and "people envy me." But I had this void I didn't know how to fill. I tried to fill it with all the wrong

things until I said, "It is about God. It is about relationships."
When I finally realized that, I knew I had the answer.

JUDY K. HERMAN

You miss out on a sense of peace and joy by detaching from
negative emotions.

DR. EDDIE CAPPARUCC

This was a calling for me. This started because I began to
develop a relationship with God. He came to me and told me
I was going to be a counselor. At first, I didn't think I would
do that. I fought Him for two years. Finally, I gave in. I got
another master's degree and did the state work. I've never
been more at peace than I have been in the past 12 years. I get
to see God every day, and I will die in this chair.

JUDY K. HERMAN

Therapists have something deep within their souls that pushes
them to grow in their own healing journey. You're making a
difference in others' lives through your counselor's chair. For
me, I'm less in my counselor's chair and more providing
therapy services outdoors through retreats. Of course, I'm
also on-stage presenting keynotes and workshops beyond the
four walls of my counseling office.

As we close, do you have a piece of advice you would give to
a couple who is beginning to realize they have issues in their
relationship?

DR. EDDIE CAPPARUCCI

I would tell them that I know it looks hopeless and like there
is no solution. I would tell them I understand that they don't
see a way out. Everybody's there in the beginning. There is a

way out. It's going to take time. It's going to be painful. But people can come out on the other side to a place they never could have imagined. Their relationship will look different than what they had before. They will be able to love, honor, and connect with their spouses. This will bring them a sense of joy beyond what I can describe.

SUMMARY

1. Sexual addiction is an intimacy disorder based on unresolved childhood pain points.

2. It normally takes 18 months to 5 years to recover from betrayal.

3. Priority is personal transformation over saving the marriage.

This has been such an insightful chapter about going deeper in order to create a better life beyond addictions. Dr. Capparucci gives us understanding about the drivers of addictions which requires increased self-awareness. He invites us to live more intentionally and take risks of growth in order to live our better lives. All this reminds me of our need to breathe fresh A.I.R. Awareness, Intentionality, and Risks. This is an acronym I use often from the stage and in the counseling room. For example:

1. Awareness – He shared about how our unresolved childhood pain points have power in our adult lives that invites addictive behavior. It's necessary to become aware of our unresolved childhood points.

2. Intentionality –We need to plan and be willing to sit with emotional distress in order to keep from avoidance or numbing out.

3. Risks of growth – It's a risk to let go of an agenda to save the relationship and move into the unknown. Through his personal story, he gives us hope that there is a new and better life on the other side.

To watch this interview along with other relationship resources, go to relationshipswithpurpose.com for your free toolkit.

 **Dr. Eddie Capparucci** is a Christian counselor and coach certified in treating problematic sexual behaviors. He has worked with professional athletes and television personalities among his many clients.

Dr. Capparucci is the creator of the *Inner Child Model* for treating Problematic Sexual Behaviors, a unique approach that focuses on identifying unresolved childhood pain points and teaching individuals how to process emotional distress in healthy ways. His treatment method has been endorsed by many leaders in this field.

TO CONTACT DR. CAPPARUCCI

✉ edcappa@gmail.com

🔗 https://abundantlifecounselingga.com/

SECRETS TO ENDING RELATIONSHIPS
FOR A BETTER LIFE

CHAPTER 8

HOW TO LIVE HAPPILY
EVEN AFTER

• • • • • • • •

Conscious Uncoupling
with Katherine Woodward Thomas

JUDY K. HERMAN

You are an incredible woman who has made a deep impact on my life. When I read your book, *Conscious Uncoupling*[1], I was going through my own conscious uncoupling.

KATHERINE WOODWARD THOMAS

That really touches me. It always moves my heart to hear how much of a difference I can make. As therapists, we spend a lot of time on Zoom and on the phone. It's nice to hear how meaningful that has been. It's touching.

JUDY K. HERMAN

I struggled with imposter syndrome when I wrote my book, *Beyond Messy Relationships*. I didn't know many therapists who were being that authentic. When I read your book, it felt like I had found my soul sister. You helped me realize I wasn't alone.

KATHERINE WOODWARD THOMAS

My friend, Polly Young-Eisendrath wrote a book called *Love Between Equals*.[2] In it she argues that we are experiencing the rapid transformation of relationships. In fact, Stephanie Coontz[3] argues that relationships have changed more in the last 30 years than they did in the 3,000 years prior to that. Polly points out that we are moving from a role-based hierarchical model into a nature-based model where both people hold power in the relationship.

Our expectations are radically different than the expectations in a role-based relationship. Polly recognizes that we aren't the people we must be to have a nature-based relationship go well. We don't have that as part of our development.

JUDY K. HERMAN

That's an interesting concept about the difference between a role-based hierarchical model verses a nature-based model with equal partnership. Share more about that.

KATHERINE WOODWARD THOMAS

Most of us weren't raised in households where we saw that modeled. Parents had a different kind of connection. Many people had parents who were getting divorced during the divorce revolution of the 1970s. We didn't have good models to show that we could bring conscious completion to a relationship in a way that created cohesion for everyone.

When we saw our parents' marriages end, it was like a wrecking ball was taken to their relationship. That caused many of us to live with a lot of confusion.

For those of us who are on the front lines of the conversation, we need to stay humble and recognize we don't have all the answers. It's helpful to know some of the questions to ask. That's what I'm finding.

JUDY K. HERMAN

There is movement from the tribal/survival hierarchical model of marriage toward equal partnership in nature-based relationships. In your holistic view, you acknowledge that we are designed for connection. Even the title, *Conscious Uncoupling,* is not a flippant idea. Rather you address divorce in such a compassionate way. You invite people to do their inner work.

KATHERINE WOODWARD THOMAS

I tried to make it simple and elegant. I wanted my book to be accessible. Sometimes people think they must be in therapy for 10 years to be deep. But I don't think any of us have 10 years to spare before we start living a happy and productive life.

The state of the world right now is elevating our need to show up in our strength, wisdom, depth, and capacity. We need to be able to shine our light. We need good relationships to be our best selves. To do that we need to think about how long we need to work on healing before we can have a great relationship.

I wanted to find the bottom of what felt like a bottomless pit created by my mom and dad. On this journey I discovered, while it's important to go back and connect the dots with our history, healing is in a different domain than transformation.

JUDY K. HERMAN
Please share more about the difference between healing and transformation.

KATHERINE WOODWARD THOMAS
There could be things that happened in our past that we will work on healing our whole lives. But we must stop duplicating those wounds, so we don't hurt ourselves over and over.

Many people feel like they married someone just like their mother or father. The secret is to take a stand for a future that's unlike anything you've ever known before.

JUDY K. HERMAN
We need to stand for a different future because focus on the past actually duplicates wounds.

KATHERINE WOODWARD THOMAS
I am a fan of happy and healthy love. I am committed to having that. I have no idea how to create that. It would be a different version of myself than who I know myself to be.

The moment you have a future you can commit to and be intentional about, you start to realize your relationship issues occur because of missing development. I don't know how to have the boundaries or how to self-regulate in a way to have a good cohesive relationship.

We're missing development, which is why we repeat patterns. We aren't repeating patterns to heal. When we repeat patterns, we feel wounded again. That's the value of having a future.

JUDY K. HERMAN

Envisioning a different future is the path toward transformation. I'm thinking that includes developing character and attitudes that are more life-giving.

KATHERINE WOODWARD THOMAS

Yes, it involves building character, skills, and capabilities. Love is unconditional, but relationships aren't. Because relationships depend upon a conditional phenomenon called trust. People must have good character to build trust. Character is a big part of it.

JUDY K. HERMAN

Relationships are dependent on conditions of trust even though love is unconditional. That's where good character and trustworthiness are crucial.

On another note, would you explain how even the words we use matter? For example, I don't like to say "Ex" in reference to former spouses.

KATHERINE WOODWARD THOMAS

"Ex" is a violent word. "Ex" makes us think of words like excommunicate and ax. There is a hostility to the word. I like a softer landing. Even if you look up the word divorce, you learn the root of the word is about separation and division. You're no longer together. We need to learn how to do things more consciously.

JUDY K. HERMAN

Yes, we need to be aware and nurture softer landings in our language and attitudes.

KATHERINE WOODWARD THOMAS

Many of us grew up damaged from the divorce of our parents. That's my story. You can spend years in therapy trying to sort through the hornet's nest *that* created. Let's find a new way for our children.

Buckminster Fuller said, "If you want to reform something, it's best to just create an alternative." [4] I like alternatives. Conscious uncoupling leads to a "wasband" instead of an "ex."

I couldn't figure out the word for ex-wife. But somebody used the term "Waswife." Constance Ahrons, who wrote the book, *The Good Divorce*[5] started the conscious divorce movement. She was so progressive in her thinking. She has also been divorced twice. She had the idea of binuclear families. In *Conscious Uncoupling* we call it "a happily even after family."

In an expanded family, it's important for the separated families to get together. Both my "wasband" and I are with new partners. And we have family meetings with our daughter and my partner. Sometimes we just exchange gifts. It's a nice cohesive feeling. For many years we did holidays together. Our daughter is in college now, and we both moved, so it's no longer viable. Having a good feeling about those folks and keeping them a part of our family made it so my daughter doesn't have to leave one family for another.

JUDY K. HERMAN

"Happily even after" feels more cohesive. Rather than divided, it's a feeling of belonging when separated families can get together to celebrate special occasions.

KATHERINE WOODWARD THOMAS

I love it when people do conscious uncoupling *before* they get divorced. Many people tell me they wish they had known the process before they divorced because they would have been able to make changes that would have made their marriage viable.

Many people recouple because of this program. The program teaches certain skills that help couples manage breakdowns in the relationship in ways that can deepen into intimacy. We can deepen the bond as opposed to harming it.

JUDY K. HERMAN

This is helpful to know that couples can manage breakdowns in ways that can actually deepen their bond.

KATHERINE WOODWARD THOMAS

Conscious uncoupling is *not* just another name for divorce. It is the recognition of where we are collectively in our development that's not aligned with common culture.

We still have these primitive reactions to separation. Someone leaving feels like life and death. These feelings engage our somatic selves in kind of a hormonal overload. Our brains and bodies go on high alert. They go to war. It's like life and death is at stake.

If you lived 1,000 years ago it probably *was* life and death for you to leave your community or tribe. You *would* probably die. You would not last long without the tribe. Our bodies and brains still have the same reaction to the ending of a relationship. Everything in us is hardwired to stay connected. And when people go from a positive bond to a negative bond, it's the trick of nature to keep us bonded. Hate is just as engaged as love in our own psyche.

JUDY K. HERMAN

We still have primitive reactions to separation because it really was life and death 1,000 years ago. That's why we are hardwired to stay together.

KATHERINE WOODWARD THOMAS

Conscious uncoupling engages inner development. The first three steps are all internal. The inner development allows us to do this in a way that matches our spiritual principles and ethics. We just haven't built the capacity for it, yet.

JUDY K. HERMAN

You mentioned the trick of nature keeping us bonded through both love and hate. Many people stay in toxic marriages because they think it's best for the kids.

KATHERINE WOODWARD THOMAS

There are studies that show we associate truancy, promiscuity, and drug use with divorce and broken families. But if you look at the research, those things reflect a war between two parents, whether or not they're married.

It's important to transition your family in a cohesive way with no break in belonging. There should be no covert pulling for your child to choose sides. The children shouldn't feel like they need to pick one family over the other. They are constantly in a state of grief, and they're disoriented about home.

When you tear a family apart, you basically leave your child homeless. This can happen in an intact, legally married family.

JUDY K. HERMAN

There's weight in that statement, "when you tear a family apart, you basically leave your child homeless." This work of conscious uncoupling is so crucial.

KATHERINE WOODWARD THOMAS

And it can happen with bird nesting, which is the practice of the parents rotating who lives in one physical home with the children each week. Bird nesting is a great idea. But if the parents are still at war with each other that home doesn't feel like a home.

As therapists we know our true home is our relational field. Parents need to figure out how to keep their homes constructed for their children. This requires an entirely different skillset unlike anything we've ever seen modeled.

JUDY K. HERMAN

Even with ending a marriage, we can help our children feel that sense of belonging rather than being "homeless." Our true home is our relational field.

KATHERINE WOODWARD THOMAS

The first three steps of conscious uncoupling are internal. When we get to steps four and five, we're on the court learning how to deal with the other person.

You're figuring out how to transition the relationship from one form to another in a way that makes sense to you and your whole community. Relationships don't belong to two people. They belong to a community of people.

JUDY K. HERMAN

This is a profound concept. "Relationships don't belong to two people. They belong to a community of people." Please share about the first three internal steps.

KATHERINE WOODWARD THOMAS

The first step is to *find emotional freedom*. The inner sanctuary is a very important part of that.

Many of us feel overwhelmed all the time and some can't get out of bed or function at all. People are running around thinking the best way to get over someone is to get under someone new while trying to manage difficult emotions.

The *inner sanctuary of safety* is about learning to hold whatever moves through you from a deeper center. And you know, that no matter what, you are okay.

You ask yourself to take your negative emotions (depression, sorrow, and rage) and turn them into a positive force for change. For example, the feeling of rage might be the feeling of deserving respect waking up inside of you.

JUDY K. HERMAN

The first step is to *find emotional freedom* which includes the *inner sanctuary of safety*. This involves learning to turn negative emotions into a positive force for change.

KATHERINE WOODWARD THOMAS

The key to doing that is learning how to hold what you're experiencing without collapsing into overly identifying with that experience and becoming the emotion. It's not just about feeling those feelings. It's about being able to label a feeling.

JUDY K. HERMAN

Labeling feelings helps us to avoid overly identifying with the emotion or experience.

KATHERINE WOODWARD THOMAS

I teach people a practice that came from Stephen Gilligan's self-relations therapy. [6] He says people should be turning towards the self, and the body, and asking how you are feeling. Then name that feeling and mirror it back. Doing that clears up your mind and allows you to figure out why you're making this about yourself.

JUDY K. HERMAN

The practice is turning inward and asking how you're feeling. Then you name the feeling and mirror it back.

Share more about step two: *Reclaim your power and your life.*

KATHERINE WOODWARD THOMAS

When you're really traumatized, your psyche is overwhelmed, and you begin to ruminate on things. You tell yourself the story over and over again in excruciating detail. Generally, you tell it from a place of victimization, because somebody else behaved very badly and you were victimized. You can't deny that.

However, if you can look at even just the 3% that *is* your fault, you're beginning to take accountability, which is self-responsibility. It might be as simple as looking at the consequences of giving up your power and why you were motivated to do that.

JUDY K. HERMAN

The psyche is overwhelmed when a person is traumatized. Yet that self-responsibility helps reclaim your power.

KATHERINE WOODWARD THOMAS

That leads into step three which is *breaking the pattern and healing your heart*. This is where you discover the underlying beliefs you've had since childhood about relationships. I call that your "source fracture story." It's the original break in your heart. It's how you prescribe meaning to your breakup.

You might think, "I'll always be alone. No one will ever love me," or "I'm not good enough." You create the meaning of your emotional center this way.

One of the first things I ask people is, "How old are you?" It's the younger part of you that wants to react this way. It's not the totality of you.

As an adult you might be a great friend, a great parent, or a very competent professional. Think about those accomplishments. Then ask yourself, "are you good enough?" You must learn how to mentor yourself and wake up from that trance.

Look at how you could show up if you were emotionally centered. I take people through a step-by-step process. The first three steps deal entirely with internal development. This kind of internal development can change relationships. They start showing up differently.

JUDY K. HERMAN

Step three is *breaking the pattern and healing your heart.*

Identifying your source fracture story brings to light old childhood beliefs and meanings about yourself and relationships. Then it's important to have a more realistic and wholesome view of yourself. That way you can show up differently in your relationships.

This seems like progressive work. Do people need to do the steps more than once? Or can they move through them and move on?

KATHERINE WOODWARD THOMAS

Ending marriage is difficult. First, you're in a court system. Then you're adjusting holidays. Then your "Wasband" is dating someone new and he introduces your kids to his new girlfriend.

It's always a process. You can revert back to these practices. But this kind of work has a North Star you're working towards. Nobody does conscious uncoupling perfectly. Conscious uncoupling is like using the bumpers at the bowling alley. When you're having a hard time in your relationship, pick up my book. Use it as a bumper. And then course correct.

JUDY K. HERMAN

These steps are a process you can go back to like your North Star. As a review, the first three steps include:

Step one: Find emotional freedom.
Step two: Reclaim your power and your life.
Step three: Break the pattern, heal your heart.

What is the fourth step?

KATHERINE WOODWARD THOMAS

Step four, which is my favorite step, is *becoming a love alchemist*. It's when you begin to repair the relationship. Likely, some degree of damage has been done, and we must clear the field, so we aren't walking around with a residue of resentment or guilt.

We must be in a clear field with the other person. I offer a way to do that. I look at realigning their intention with their relationship.

In step one, we set a personal intention. For example, I'm going to outgrow who I've known myself to be. So, my relationships are going to be healthy, respectful, and mutual in the future. I'm only going to be intimate with people who have the capacity to love me. I'm not going to think I can make it up for both of us.

In step four you might discover you two are great co-parents. But you don't want to be connected to your former partner. Conscious uncoupling doesn't advocate for friendship because friendship is earned. When someone has shown poor character, it is best to stay disconnected.

Moving forward, you might carry that person with you as your dark guru and the person who taught you so much. Bless them, thank them, and send them on their way. Then you're not walking around with unresolved resentment.

JUDY K. HERMAN

That's a shift in perspective. A former partner who has shown poor character can be a dark guru rather than a friend. Friendship requires earned trustworthiness. Instead, appreciate what you learned in the darkness of the relationship and let go of resentment.

KATHERINE WOODWARD THOMAS

My favorite part of step four is the generosity piece where I invite people to be generous, to generate something new. This generosity could initiate a new era in the relationship that's built on mutuality, respect, and friendliness.

You might never be best friends. But you want to make sure there is a clear and friendly field between yourself and the person you're co-parenting with. This is repair work that needs to be done. I advocate for generous gestures of repair.

JUDY K. HERMAN

Generosity can create a clear and friendly field between two former spouses. What a gift to the children! Step four is *becoming a love alchemist* in which you create a different relationship without the residue of guilt and resentment.

How *can* former spouses both consciously uncouple when they couldn't agree on other things? Does anyone automatically think they are going to do conscious uncoupling together?

KATHERINE WOODWARD THOMAS

Many people think that, but it usually doesn't happen. 95% of people do it alone. Even when people do it together, they're doing it separately. I tell people not to expect that they will be on the same page. For example, one person might stay on step one for a month. And the other is already on step four by week two. People have their own pacing.

This is an unusual program created by a marriage and family therapist about how to separate. You're creating separateness and spaciousness in your relationship and coming home to yourself.

Some people go back and forth. Some do recouple.

If they go back, they bring a greater capacity to self-regulate and a greater capacity to be responsible for their own choices and actions. They take responsibility for those actions and what they create for the other person. They understand how to make amends to the other person when they have wronged them.

A lot of us think if we've made a mistake, and we've hurt someone's feelings, if we explain the psychology behind the action, that should clear the air. But it doesn't. It does the opposite. It shows why the person is damaged. And you think they will always wound you this way.

JUDY K. HERMAN
Explaining why we made a mistake or wronged the other person is not the same as making amends. But, practicing the steps helps people create a greater capacity to self-regulate and be responsible for their own choices and actions.

KATHERINE WOODWARD THOMAS
People must learn the art of mirroring the damage their unconscious behavior does and then learn how to make amends for that. We talk about that in step four. It's the part where they clear the air between them.

They learn how they show up inside of their *original source fracture story* when they get triggered. The ability to wake themselves up and look for a deeper truth is an important part to step four. They will begin to show up in healthier ways that are more generative of the relationship they want to have. All these things can happen in conscious uncoupling.

JUDY K. HERMAN

Would you explain more about the *original fracture story?* This seems like a big piece of the process.

KATHERINE WOODWARD THOMAS

Collectively, we are very unconscious as to how *I am the source of my own experience.* It's very covert. For example, things happen that bring me to my trigger place when I'm all alone. Then I think that everyone always leaves me. If I think I'm all alone and everyone always leaves me, I never get my needs met.

That's the consciousness I'm walking in. In other words, I've collapsed into that self, rather than concentrating on what's true which is: *I have the power to generate connection.*

JUDY K. HERMAN

The *original fracture story* is a magnet for collapsing into the self rather than aligning with the truth.

KATHERINE WOODWARD THOMAS

Instead of going in that direction, I'm collapsing into my four-year-old perspective. And I'm acting from there. I'm going to be self-sufficient and not ask for help. I'll get my safety from being the one who is always giving without expecting much in return. Then I'm going to start relationships with people who

don't have a lot to give. Maybe I give myself away too easily.
I self-abandon to prevent people from leaving me.

JUDY K. HERMAN
That's a clear example of an original fracture story.

KATHERINE WOODWARD THOMAS
There is an entire system for how I relate to myself, to others,
and to life. If I mistake it for my personality or my issues, it
generates from that core consciousness.

I must look at how I am the source of the dynamics in my
relationship. I can't victimize myself by saying something
vague like, "Oh, I married my narcissistic father again." Then,
I have no access to change.

JUDY K. HERMAN
If we don't identify that *original facture story*, we can still get
caught up in the old pattern.

KATHERINE WOODWARD THOMAS
It's a slippery slope. You get stuck even if you connect the dots
between what happened in your past to what's happening in
your present *without* seeing the piece where you are
perpetuating this to happen in the present.

If I allow myself to be victimized by what my father did 40
years ago, I'll still be stuck in the self that was created as a
response to that dynamic. That's the case even if he's owned
it and made amends, or even if he passed away 20 years ago.

JUDY K. HERMAN
I can see why just connecting the dots between the past and

present is not enough. Rather changing our perspective and taking responsibility are necessary for transformation.

KATHERINE WOODWARD THOMAS

Where we put our attention grows. If we keep going backwards unpacking the story and bringing our client into over-identification with the self that was formed in their trauma, we're solidifying the self that formed there. It's important not to dwell too long on the past.

People must do the trauma work and reclaim their bodies. They need to see where they clearly split off from themselves. It's important work. We are looking at what *they* made it mean about themselves. They need to figure out the self they crafted as a response to their trauma or an ongoing experience. They need to figure out how to wake themselves from that trance.

JUDY K. HERMAN

We need to realize that the past doesn't define us. Is waking up from the trance about changing the meanings about ourselves?

KATHERINE WOODWARD THOMAS

I tell people that they are never going to get rid of that part of themselves. They may always get trigged by certain things. They can develop the ability to stop, take a deep breath, and ask themselves what they are assuming to be true right now.

They can figure out where they are centered. Because wherever they are centered at their level of identity is where they will respond from. It's how they'll generate their relationships and how they generate their life.

Relationships are dynamic. They're always shifting and changing.

JUDY K. HERMAN

It's simple and profound. We can learn to stop, take a deep breath, and ask ourselves what we assume to be true.

KATHERINE WOODWARD THOMAS

Taking these steps is about helping all of us develop the capacity to stand in what's true. It's a way we can feel in our bodies, relate to our younger selves, and go back and mentor that self to have true meaning.

For me it's like the image of mothers out in the field with their babies strapped to their bodies, so they can go about their day while they hold their baby.

The other image is getting the child out of the driver's seat and putting her in a loving car seat in the backseat where she is safe. You can talk to her. But the grownup is driving the car and the relationships.

JUDY K. HERMAN

These are great images. What advice do you want to give to anyone reading this?

KATHERINE WOODWARD THOMAS

First, start with the future that you're committed to creating. Always start with the future and then let that inform the choices you make and the actions you take to find your way. Stephen Covey[7] and John Gottman[8] both talked about how people should start at the end.

For example, when you start a fight ask yourself how you want it to end. Many of us are good at looking backwards to find out why we are the way we are. But I think we're too weak when we look at the future.

We need to not only look at what we want but what we want to become. Then use that as your North Star. Organize yourself to become who you need to be to manifest that future.

SUMMARY

1. Conscious uncoupling helps families transition through divorce in a cohesive way with no break in belonging.

2. Studies of children with truancy, promiscuity, and drug use reflect more on the war between two parents whether or not they are married (rather than on the effects of divorce.)

3. Our true home is our relational field. It's possible to create a sense of safety, freedom and belonging.

JUDY'S CHAPTER TAKE-AWAYS

Talking with Katherine felt so validating for me on many levels. It's true that we will meet our future selves. Yet we're so good at looking back with what we already have experienced and known. We're more comfortable with what we've known rather than strengthening our imaginations to create a better, yet unfamiliar life. She reminds us that it's so vital to start with the end in mind.

Another point is the value of experiencing strong negative emotions. Rather than over-identifying with them, they are temporary messengers to our souls. She helps us decipher those messages when she says to turn them into a positive force for change.

Of course, I appreciate the analogy of mothers in the fields with babies strapped to their bodies. Care and nurture the younger self who shows up occasionally. Then get back to being the adult.

This is a chapter you'll want to re-read, and highlight. You'll be able to watch as it's included in your free toolkit: go to relationshipswithpurpose.com

Katherine Woodward Thomas is *the New York Times* bestselling author of *Conscious Uncoupling: 5 Steps to Living Happily Even After* and *Calling in "The One": 7 Weeks to Attracting the Love of Your Life.*[9] She is also an award-winning marriage and family psychotherapist.

Over the past two decades, Katherine has taught hundreds of thousands of people from all over the world how to create conscious, loving relationships and to realize the higher potentials all their connections hold for health and happiness.

Katherine trains and certifies people to become Conscious Uncoupling Coaches and provides ongoing supervision and development to her community of coaches from around the world.

TO CONTACT KATHERINE

✉ support@katherinewoodwardthomas.com

🔗 https://katherinewoodwardthomas.com/

CHAPTER 9

HOW TO EXTRACT CLARITY FROM EMOTIONAL ABUSE

• • • • • • • •

Flying Free
with Natalie Hoffman

JUDY K. HERMAN

You have made such a difference for women who are in confusing marriages. They are dealing with covert emotional and spiritual abuse. Would you share more about that?

NATALIE HOFFMAN

I used to say that one out of every three women in Christian environments are in a covert abusive relationship. Now, I think it's closer to half. There are no statistics on it because covert abuse is under the radar and difficult to understand. People figure it out by talking to other people who've experienced it and can put words to it.

I have an emotional abuse quiz. It asks you questions about what you experience in your marriage. Many people on the outside of your marriage might think your experience is not a big deal if they only look at one little behavior. Maybe a little behavior wouldn't be a big deal if it happened once in a great while.

But with covert abuse, as Patrick Doyle[1] said, it's "a death by a million cuts." The behaviors may be small, but they are patterns that happen repeatedly. They never stop.

JUDY K. HERMAN

Covert abuse can be so confusing. In contrast, physical abuse can be easily identified. If your partner hits you, gives you bruises, or traps you in a room, people can see that these are abusive actions.

You bring clarity in your book, *Is It Me?*[2] You described your definition of hidden emotional domestic abuse. "It is the secret, regular, and repeated cruel mistreatment of the inner emotions and heart of another person living within the same home."

NATALIE HOFFMAN

They're targeting the emotions of another human being. They're using emotional manipulation. It may be guilt manipulation or shame to control that person and get them to do what they want them to do.

It works really well on Christian women especially who have a higher guilty conscience that flares up very easily. They want to follow God, do what's right, obey the Bible, and make their husband happy. So, it's very easy for a Christian man, if he understands all of this, to use that against his partner to get her to discount her own perspectives and ideas and to feel a lot of shame and guilt.

JUDY K. HERMAN

A Christian woman with a higher guilty conscience can easily fall victim to emotional manipulation. The origin of these patterns is likely part of a bigger system than the couple.

Are the "abusers" doing it on purpose? Or is this learned behavior passed down from what they witnessed in their family? Do you think emotional abuse is something modeled from our parents' relationship?

NATALIE HOFFMAN

I think some of them are aware of what they are doing. And they are doing it on purpose to be malicious. Many of them, however, do it because it works.

You get married to someone. And then you start noticing. If you want something, all you have to do is make a little sideways jab, be passive aggressive, or make an implication that makes the other person try to fix it. Then, it makes you feel better.

I don't even know that they're consciously thinking their abuse tactic works. It's just human nature to do what's pragmatic and works for us. If someone wants their way and he knows he can get it by guilting or manipulating his partner, he's going to do that.

It stems from an inward attitude of entitlement that already exists in the abusive person. They are already like that. That's who they are as a human being.

That's why people like this don't want to be with someone who has strong boundaries and who will say "no." If this kind of abusive person meets a woman, and she tells him "no," or is very confident about her own perspective and opinions, the abuser won't be attracted to her. He can't manipulate that kind of individual.

JUDY K. HERMAN

The abusive person is attracted to someone he can manipulate. We often think of the abusive person as the man and the victim as the woman. Does it go both ways?

NATALIE HOFFMAN

It definitely goes both ways. I know couples where the woman is the abusive one. I'm aware of that. But all my work is with female victims. So, I usually assume that is the gender dynamic. If a woman comes to me first, I'll assume she's telling the truth. But it does go both ways.

JUDY K. HERMAN

Women grew up with stories like Cinderella, Prince Charming, and Sleeping Beauty. A woman might see a potential spouse with strong leadership skills. And she has always wanted to be with a leader. Then that idea is built into the patriarchal church systems. The man is supposed to be the spiritual leader. Can you speak to why women might be drawn to this?

NATALIE HOFFMAN

Complementarian thinking is the idea that men were created to be leaders and that they were naturally designed to be leaders. Whereas women were created to be followers and naturally designed to play a certain role.

This thinking is very limited in its understanding of nature and it's understanding of God. It became popular in some Christian circles. And it specifically grooms women and makes them believe it's part of God's plan to not have boundaries or to not have perspectives. If they do have perspective, they think it's below a male's perspective.

JUDY K. HERMAN

It's helpful to have labels like "complementarian thinking" to describe these roles. Otherwise, it's taken for granted.

NATALIE HOFFMAN

Christian women are especially susceptible to this kind of thinking. And it has spread out to the culture at large. Throughout the history of the world, people have been very misogynistic.[3] Even now culture is starting to come around. And people are having conversations about how this is not correct.

People still imagine families the way they were in the 1950s. The dad went to work, and the mom stayed home. This only happened for a period. This was not the norm throughout history. But Christians today now think of those years as the golden years. It's because women were living out their God given roles while men lived out their God given roles.

This idea is just hogwash. If you look at history, it doesn't even compute. In all of history, however, we can see misogyny. For example, most women would rather live today than live 100 years ago.

JUDY K. HERMAN

Examining history and seeing how it's affected us today, has perpetuated some of these same stereotypes. It's so damaging, isn't it?

NATALIE HOFFMAN

Yes, and that is what I see in the Church, in general. There are some good churches out there that are healthy. They understand that men and women, while different, have equal perspectives and are equal before God.

Yet, there are many pockets and denominations of Christianity that still think men should be in charge. This is where most of the abuse is taking place. There is a huge movement for these women to get educated because they have been isolated. They've been told what books to read and what pastors to listen to. And people who disagree are heretical and shouldn't be listened to.

This is what nations and countries do when they're using propaganda to control the thinking of the people. This is what the church is doing to control the thinking of women and keep them in a place of subservience and oppression willingly.

Women are staying there willingly. They want to stay there because they've been brainwashed into thinking this is what God wants. They think if God wants this, it's what they need to do. This is a lie from the devil. Now, I'm seeing this mentality turn around. There is a huge movement of people who are standing up, saying this is satanic, and refusing to stand for it.

JUDY K. HERMAN

Share your background story that gives you such passion for this work.

NATALIE HOFFMAN

I grew up in a very conservative Christian home. We were immersed in the Bill Gothard movement.[4] I used to go to his seminars in the '70s and '80s. I married a man who was a brand-new Christian at the time.

I could see the problems. But I thought it was my job to be the wind beneath his wings, help him, and be his helpmate. Then everything was going to be great. I got involved in the homeschooling community. We had nine children. We used the Bill Gothard curriculum for four years. I was heavily into vision forum.

My marriage was painful and confusing from the start. Six months into my marriage, I was sick to my stomach because I realized I made a big mistake. And there was no way out. I did not believe in divorce. So, I made the best of it. I had nine children. I've loved God since I was seven years old. I have been passionate about my relationship with God since then.

Eventually I tried to get help from the church in various ways at different times throughout our marriage. Then I found Leslie Vernick's book[5] while pregnant with my last child. Desperate, I wanted to kill myself.

I went to a hotel, and I was racked in sobs all night long. I wanted to drown in the bathtub. But my son was due in about three weeks. And I knew I couldn't kill my baby. The next day I took my laptop and went to a coffee shop and started Googling phrases like *passive aggressive.*

I didn't know about emotional abuse. I had never heard that term before. So, I started Googling and I found a book called

Who's Pushing Your Buttons? by Henry Cloud and John Townsend.[6]

It was *about* emotional abuse, but it wasn't using that terminology. I was underlining the whole book and learning there was a language for what I had been experiencing. When I read Leslie Vernick's book, *The Emotionally Destructive Marriage*,[7] I immediately hired her to coach me.

During this time, I had an in-home separation from my husband. Leslie tries to empower women to be able to make their own decisions. A lot of Christian women want to stay in their relationship. They don't want to get divorced. At first, I thought that was what I wanted. Vernick's book leans in that direction. So, it was perfect for me at the time.

Eventually, however, I made my husband leave the home and we were separated for almost two years. During that time, I realized he wasn't going to change, and I could not be with him anymore. I had two choices: kill myself or get a divorce. I decided God wanted me to get a divorce, and not kill myself.

JUDY K. HERMAN

It's important to realize that your mental health is of utmost importance. How many kids did you have at home during this time?

NATALIE HOFFMAN

I had nine kids in the house at the time. I was still homeschooling then. I did eventually put my kids in a variety of different places depending on what they needed. Then my youngest ended up having autism.

The next five years of my life was a nightmare trying to get out and learn new things. That's when I started implementing boundaries. I started seeing I was a worthwhile person. Before, my feelings of worthiness were at rock bottom. I thought I was a piece of refuse on the ground.

I do not believe Jesus teaches this. Christian teaching, however, makes the problem worse because they tell you you're such a dirty, rotten little worm. And God can't even look at you because of how gross you are. I had internalized that and bought into that to the extreme. I thought it was humility.

How will we ever make an impact on the world when we are shut down and curled up in the fetal position on our bathroom floor, trying to survive the next day? I don't think that's what Jesus Christ came to offer us. I think he came to set us free from that.

JUDY K. HERMAN
I so agree. I've come to believe embracing our worthiness of dignity, love and respect is a foundational truth. How did your transformation affect your kids?

NATALIE HOFFMAN
When you're in that relationship you're trying to make it work. You create a pseudo stability. You're dancing along with your partner and you're doing your part to keep him happy. That keeps the equilibrium in the relationship.

Then you start standing up for yourself and setting boundaries. You're saying, "yes," I will do this, but "no," I won't do that. "My perspective is different from yours." Then you start experiencing *that* kickback. Suddenly, we've created an unstable situation for the kids. The whole family feels it.

JUDY K. HERMAN

That can create a lot of confusion when there's equilibrium with the toxic patterns. Then moving toward healthy boundaries brings instability to the family.

NATALIE HOFFMAN

At the time, I didn't have a lot of mind management skills to help organize my brain around that. Now I do. And I help other women with that.

I was experiencing symptoms of complex Post-Traumatic Stress Disorder.[8] The symptoms are very similar to borderline personality disorder.[9] People get hysterical and start feeling like they're going crazy. People start communicating in ways that are very desperate, loud, and out of control. I was doing that while in that unstable place. It was important for me to go through that phase to get help for myself.

JUDY K. HERMAN

Yes, it's so important to get support.

NATALIE HOFFMAN

Once the relationship was done and he was out of the house, I started to settle. I was able to have the emotional capacity to go back to what I was doing before and help my children and hold space for their emotions.

When you're trying to get out of a relationship, it's going to get a lot worse before it gets better. Many people say to me that they feel they are making the wrong choice. Because everything is getting worse.

But that's exactly what's supposed to happen. You're supposed to destabilize the whole thing. The house of cards must fall before you can rebuild it. There are a lot of books out there about emotional abuse. But mine focuses on the religious fallout that can happen. My church excommunicated me as well.

When you're in environments of abuse, the whole thing collapses. You need to be validated and supported through that. Because it is traumatic with a capital T. You're losing everything.

JUDY K. HERMAN

It's important to expect things to get worse before getting better. That's what happens when you're in environments of abuse. And it's common to question whether or not you're making the right choice.

NATALIE HOFFMAN

You're also a mother. So, you need to be able to help your children with what they're going through. They're trying to process the fact that Mom and Dad are separated. And they might get a divorce. And their whole lives are falling apart while you are trying to figure out who in the world you are, *what* in the world you're doing, and *what* your future is going to look like.

It's pure terror and chaos for a while. In the program we help women walk through that chaos. We walk through it with them. They have the support and tools they need to get through it in a way that's much healthier than what I went through. It's going to fall apart, but hopefully they won't feel alone in it like I did.

JUDY K. HERMAN

It is a terrifying experience. It's amazing you paved the way. It took such courage to do what you did. Share about the Sisterhood program and what you offer.

NATALIE HOFFMAN

It's called *The Flying Free Sisterhood*[10]. We like to call ourselves butterflies. In my program I have courses and things you can take. I do group coaching each week. Everyone gets to hear other people get coached.

We're all going through the same things so it's very applicable. It's convenient because we put everything on a private podcast. Theoretically, you don't even have to log into the membership site. You can just get the private podcast and open it when there is a new update. You can listen to it while you're doing laundry or the dishes. It doesn't necessarily have to cut into your time.

These women are under so much pressure emotionally. We try to make it easy.

JUDY K. HERMAN

You know what they are going through. Share more about the process.

NATALIE HOFFMAN

I want to help women have the time and capacity to hold what I'm saying without being affected by the brain fog. It's very difficult to think clearly when you're in that kind of chaos.

I remember that I needed to hear things over and repeatedly just to understand them. They were such new ideas and concepts that I had never heard before. My brain was so programmed a certain way. It took a long time for me to help my brain open and hear new ideas and new thoughts. Those things changed my life once I was able to hear them and reprogram my brain in a different direction.

JUDY K. HERMAN

Repetition is so vital in reprogramming the brain for well-being.

NATALIE HOFFMAN

We have a private forum where people can interact with each other and get to know each other. We had our very first butterfly bootcamp with over 100 women who came in person. It's great to get together in person. Because for the most part, these women are alone in their houses, and they need connection.

If they go to their church and say something, they're going to be told they are airing their husband's dirty laundry and being disrespectful and rebellious. They will be shut down and shamed. It's scary to feel like you don't have anyone who understands or knows what you're going through.

JUDY K. HERMAN

Community makes all the difference when going through such major healing. I tell my clients that there are two ways to change the structure of the brain. One is through trauma. The other is through repetition. We're choosing repetition to reinforce new and healthy ways to think.

NATALIE HOFFMAN

Listening to a lot of podcasts that are saying similar things can be helpful. Then you know it's not just one person who is saying this. There's a whole body of knowledge out there that we can expose ourselves to.

I love going down rabbit holes because I'll find someone on someone else's podcast that leads me to something else. I view that as the Holy Spirit guiding me. I believe God is conspiring in our favor and that He wants to lead us along if we are willing to be brave and go to places that are unusual or where we have never gone before.

JUDY K. HERMAN

This is a phrase worth pondering. "God is conspiring in our favor."

NATALIE HOFFMAN

Christian women are especially scared to branch out of their particular denomination or their way of thinking. We will never grow or change if we are not willing to be wrong about things. We must go through life willing to be wrong. That's how we learn.

JUDY K. HERMAN

Yes, we learn from being willing to be wrong about things. That's how our brains are designed. It's called neuroplasticity. We're designed to grow up and develop those new neural pathways to challenge our old beliefs that are no longer serving us.

We've all been programmed on so many levels. We might think "the enemy" is trying to invade our minds. But it's a "divine invitation" to grow into healthy ways of thinking and being.

Are most of the women you work with Christian? Or do you work with people in other faiths too?

NATALIE HOFFMAN

Most of them follow some version of the Christian faith. We've had a Jewish client in the past. We've had a Muslim person in the past. I don't know how many are of different faiths because not all of them have disclosed what their faith is. It doesn't matter what the faith is. If your faith has been part of what's hooked you into an abusive mindset, then that's what I help women with.

I love God and I believe God is *for* women. And I want to see women and their faith in God grow deeper and stronger and more profound. I want them to lean into the love of God. That's what will set them free.

Their faith and how their faith has abused them has put up a gargantuan, thick wall between them and God. That wall needs to be torn down. Abuse prevents them from getting to know who they are and who God created them to be. Religious abuse prevents them from getting to know who God is. We want to tear down all those walls so they can find health, hope, and healing with God.

JUDY K. HERMAN

Do you find a certain demographic of woman who experience covert and spiritual abuse?

NATALIE HOFFMAN

I'm seeing it across the board. Most of the women come out of the homeschool, conservative, patriarchal Christian movements. I grew up believing that it was wrong for a mom to have a job outside of the home. The people coming out of that are going to be mostly stay at home moms.

We do have a lot of therapists, teachers, and other caretaking roles who are in the program. They are powerful human beings. They love and care for people. That hooks them and makes them more susceptible to being manipulated by people.

Those people are easy to work with. Once the light bulb goes on, they make those connections and can heal pretty quickly because they've got a lot of tools in their toolbox. They just need to see how it applies to them and how they're letting their boundaries down or not valuing themselves as much. I feel like they get it much more quickly and their turnaround of healing is much quicker. I love that they're turning around and taking their healing to so many people because of the kind of job they have.

Moms who are in the process of healing are helping their children heal too. They're making a difference. I hear a lot of testimonies of how this transformation happened inside of them. It's changed the way they parent. Their kids have a leg up on life. Their moms learned these tools and are now able to pass them on to their kids. Their kids will be much further along than they were at 16 or 17 years old.

JUDY K. HERMAN

They are changing their branch of the family tree. It's a lot of work because there have been generations of patterns that affected their neural pathways. It's courageous and remarkable work to be in the process of breaking through these things.

I've sent clients your way, Natalie, and your programs and books are such great supplement to their therapy. You give them courage and help them move forward. There is only so much an individual therapist can do to help a woman. But when there is a whole community supporting her, it makes it easier to find the courage to change.

NATALIE HOFFMAN

Many people come in and say, "My therapist recommended this program or this book." Get individual therapy for your own personal problems. It's important to hear the truth and understand what you're experiencing. It's an issue in the Christian and religious world.

This is a global issue. All those pieces come together to help give a person the very best chances of healing and moving forward to become a world changer. I believe in the butterfly effect. When you change your life, you change the world.

JUDY K. HERMAN

How has this work changed you?

NATALIE HOFFMAN

The skills God gave me when I was born were taken and suppressed through oppression. I had to go from being a caterpillar to a butterfly. In the chrysalis, the caterpillar turns into goo, and it becomes shapeless and formless. It's just jelly in there.

If you were in an emotionally and spiritually abusive

relationship, you had to go through that too. It's the dark night of the soul. That's where all the chaos and pain happen. You don't know what your future's going to hold. But you must go through that. That's where God does that transforming work. Now, I'm finally flying.

I feel like I've been a caterpillar my whole life when I wanted to be a butterfly. It was like I was looking to the other parents for direction and help while staying in my child role.

I finally grew up for the first time in my 50s. I learned God speaks to me directly. He doesn't speak to me through a pastor or through the worship leader. I can make adult decisions. I can have confidence and certainty in my choices and my decisions. I'm also free to make mistakes and be okay with them. There's no shame in making mistakes. There's no shame in trying things and failing. That's how we learn, grow, and develop.

JUDY K. HERMAN
You can have confidence in your choices. There's no shame in making mistakes. It's our human journey to learn, grow, and develop.

NATALIE HOFFMAN
Life is still going to be great half the time and not so great for the other half. I'm finally flowing and living the life that God prepared for me. When people are in an abusive relationship, you feel like your life is wasted. When you get out and look back, it's easy to think it was a waste and you could have spent those years differently.

None of it is a waste. All of it matters. It's like a trampoline you jump on that propels you into your future. Without that trampoline launching pad, you wouldn't have the future that's in store for you.

I don't care how old you are, you have a future. I believe that we are eternal beings. You have a future here on earth. You are still a world changer in your 80s and even in your 90s. My grandmother lived to be in her 90s. My great-grandmother lived to be 104.

We are world changers no matter what stage we're at. Our past is part of the big, beautiful package of who God created us to be and how he wants us to change the world.

SUMMARY

1. Women of faith who have a higher guilty conscious can easily fall victim to emotional manipulation.

2. Those who abuse have attitudes of entitlement using emotional manipulation or shame to get their partners to do what they want.

3. Expect confusion and difficulty when breaking free from the equilibrium of ingrained toxic systems. Community support is necessary. God is conspiring for you.

If you're like me, you likely felt the intensity of Natalie's story. For some, reading this may be like a gut punch. If so, read this chapter again and take deep breaths along the way. You're not alone.

Overall, I admire Natalie's courage, stamina, and resilience and ministering to others so powerfully. You may have noticed how she uses the analogy of the butterfly as did Dr. Debi Silber in a previous chapter. With careful observations, you'll notice common themes with several guests who educate us about necessary steps toward Better Relationships and a Better Life.

What Natalie shared aligns with the growth formula of breathing fresh A.I.R. Awareness, Intentionality, and Risks of Growth. She raises *awareness* about covert emotional and spiritual abuse. She has created a program for women to be *intentional* to gain support and learn more. She offers support, mentoring and coaching for those who are ready for their *risks of growth*.

To watch this interview within your free toolkit: go to relationshipswithpurpose.com

Natalie Hoffman is the author of *Is it Me? Making Sense of Your Confusing Marriage* as well as the host of the *Flying Free* podcast.[11] She helps women of faith find hope and healing from hidden emotional and spiritual abuse. Recovery from her conservative Christian mindset led her to develop the Flying Free Sisterhood program, a private forum for survivors that offers classes, expert workshops, and weekly live coaching.

TO CONTACT NATALIE

natalie@flyingfreenow.com

https://www.flyingfreenow.com/

SECRETS TO HELP CREATE BETTER RELATIONSHIPS AND A BETTER LIFE

CHAPTER 10

HOW TO CREATE CONNECTION BEYOND CONFLICT

•••••••••

Getting the Love You Want
with Harville Hendrix & Helen LaKelly Hunt

JUDY K. HERMAN

You two have been remarkably influential in my life. It all began when I was a freshly licensed counselor deciding to do couples therapy. When I read *Getting the Love You Want[1]*, I was on the heels of divorce after a 30-year marriage and four kids. Your work runs deep in my soul, both on a professional and personal level. I just wanted, first of all, to thank you.

And for those who have never heard of Imago Therapy[2], do give us a quick description.

HARVILLE HENDRIX

Well, thank you for sharing that.

Imago Therapy is couple's therapy that focuses, not on the individual, but on couples. And it's not exclusively couples.

Single people who are interested in being in a relationship can benefit from the theory and the process. We call it relationship therapy because it also applies to people in relationships who are not couples. It works in corporations, business partners, and congregations. Fundamentally it works with two people in a dyad, whether they are married or not.

HELEN LAKELLY HUNT

Harville and I were both divorced and living in a city. He was giving speeches on something no one was giving speeches on. They were on the different stages of a relationship. I went to one of his first speeches, which was in a garage.

HARVILLE HENDRIX

Imago Therapy was invented in a garage.

HELEN LAKELLY HUNT

The garage belonged to a church member. In addition to meeting at the church, they sometimes met in a man's garage and had a speaker. People would come and sit on little metal chairs and listen to a speech. They asked Harville and he agreed.

During his presentation, he used a chalkboard. Then he said, "There are three stages of a relationship." He drew one mark and labeled it "stage one," which is *romantic attraction*. This is the stage where we think everything is great.

Then he explained that the next stage of a relationship is number two, called the *power struggle*. Everyone in stage one ends up in stage two. Then they are surprised when they experience power struggles. They didn't know that was going to happen. Then after learning a few things, everyone *can* get to stage three, which is *real love.*

JUDY K. HERMAN

The three stages of relationship that Harville taught were:

1. Romantic attraction
2. Power struggle
3. Real love

HELEN LAKELLY HUNT

Well, I thought that was pretty impressive and we started dating. And then I was training to be a therapist. I wanted to be a Jungian analyst having received my master's in counseling psychology. So, I proposed to him, and I said, "If you marry me, let's move to New York. We'll get a publisher."

I was getting a doctorate in psychology. So, I was a great thought partner at the beginning. I began to do some work that was parallel to his. My heart, however, has always been with the vision of relationships. Judy, I love the way you say it. If you have a better relationship, you have a better life. The world needs to know that.

We have a value system that tells us to be the best when we grow up. Win the debate team or win the spelling bee. Train yourself to be the best, the best, the best. And the three of us want to get out a message. If you want to have a better life, have better relationships.

JUDY K. HERMAN

Yes. Our value system of "training to be the best when we grow up" *is* a different message. The world *does* need to know that better relationships *do* make a better life.

HARVILLE HENDRIX

Helen was much more than a thought partner. That's part of her modesty. She was indispensable in the process. We were partners from the beginning. We've always had an intense relationship, negative and positive. About three weeks after we met, I was in Helen's living room, and we were having an intense negative interaction. Then she said, "Stop. One of us needs to talk while the other listens. Let's take turns talking and listening."

That was the beginning of our dialogue, and the rest is history. At that point we were in conversation about the key intervention. Dialogue became the key intervention in Imago Therapy. Therefore, everything else evolved from that and Helen has been a co-partner the whole time.

She brought ideas that I hadn't thought about. I'm a systems builder and she's intuitive. She would say, "What about this?" and I would say, "No, no, I can't see that." Then I would think about it and realize that's the next block in the theory. Or it needs to be built in.

HELEN LAKELLY HUNT

And this guy knows how to simplify the complex.

HARVILLE HENDRIX

Well, that's because it's simple.

JUDY K. HERMAN

Dialogue is the speaker-listener key intervention of Imago Therapy. I'm so thankful to be an Imago Therapist who helps couples create this emotionally safe space through dialogue skills. You've shown us that the listener is the one who chooses to get out of their world and into the speaker's world. We all long to be heard and understood.

HELEN LAKELLY HUNT

Yes, we teach couples or anyone who wants to have a better relationship how to dialogue. By the way, these skills became teachable because of Harville. He showed us how to learn it which had never been done before in history.

Before that, a psychiatrist just gave information. All the departments of psychiatry around the country medicate and isolate. Harville was part of making the relational sciences teachable.

JUDY K. HERMAN

That's a remarkable historic influence in the relational sciences, Harville. I had no idea that dialogue skills became teachable for the first time then.

Helen, share more about the need for curiosity when practicing dialogue.

HELEN LAKELLY HUNT

There was something I read in *Dan Siegel's handbook*.[3] He wrote about the dorsal lateral prefrontal cortex between the left and right brain hemispheres. Dan said, "Tolerating ambiguity is a sign of brain health." Well, I almost closed the book because I thought that was the dumbest thing I had ever read. I thought Dan was smart. Doesn't Dan know that being smart is a sign of brain health? How is tolerating ambiguity a sign of brain health?

As I read more, I learned that some people call it the Dalai Lama state. It's part of the brain between the left and right hemisphere where people wonder about things. He says it promotes neural integration.

JUDY K. HERMAN
So, it's that mystery part of the brain?

HELEN LAKELLY HUNT
Yes, it's living with mystery and wonder about the other person. The brain is the most complex organ in the universe that resides in your skull and the other person's skull.

We tell people to think of the lower brain as the crocodile that keeps you alive. It's reactive. You don't choose to live in the crocodile. But when you're hungry you eat and when you're tired you sleep. We love the crocodile brain because it does all these things to keep us alive.

It's limited in what it can do. Above the crocodile brain is the wise owl brain. This is the part of your brain that you can choose to be in. You can live your whole life in the crocodile brain. A lot of people live their whole lives reactive. They don't understand someone who is different than them.

JUDY K. HERMAN
The lower brain keeps us alive, yet it's reactive. It's the crocodile brain. The wise owl brain is above the crocodile brain. We can choose to be in the wise owl part. But most people live their whole lives reactive.

Would you give examples?

HELEN LAKELLY HUNT

We see this happening in politics. Neither party can empathize or see the other's point of view. They operate from an "I'm right, you're wrong," position. That's the way a lot of the world works. And it's the way a lot of relationships work.

You can choose to go to the neocortex, which is the owl. There are a lot of invaluable left-brain people including linear architects, doctors, and accountants. Some scientists are left and right brained. Right brain knowledge is often our gut instinct and intuitive knowledge.

JUDY K. HERMAN

Not only do we have the lower (reactive) and upper (wise) parts of the brain. But we also have the left (linear) and right (intuitive) parts of the brain.

HELEN LAKELLY HUNT

Connecting the dots between the left brain and right brain develops your ability to choose to go to the tolerating ambiguous part. Then your whole brain is working on helping your relationship succeed.

HARVILLE HENDRIX

This means that when you practice the dialogue process, it activates all the lobes of the brain in an integrative way. Through dialogue you create a better brain and better relationship.

JUDY K. HERMAN

Wow! How you interact in relationships affects your brain health.

HELEN LAKELLY HUNT

Acetylcholine, norepinephrine, serotonin are all relaxing neurochemicals. The Mayo Clinic says, people who live in the upper part of the brain, live longer, don't get sick as much, and have a healthier immune system. Your whole body is healthier if you have healthier relationships.

JUDY K. HERMAN

That's amazing! Your whole body is healthier if you have healthier relationships. With dialogue, people are learning a speaker/listener skill that activates the lobes of the brain. One person mirrors the other during reflective listening.

How important is it to practice deep breathing in order to slow down reactions during this process?

HARVILLE HENDRIX

The deep breathing is important because we are all our own energy field. Like Einstein said, "energy equals matter times the speed of light squared." I'm an energy field and Helen is an energy field. We also live in an energy field. So, there is a field between us.

The value of the left brain is that you can make sense out of your intuition. For example, let's say the energy field is like a pool of water. As Helen talks, she influences the water, and as I talk, I influence the water. How I interact with Helen makes this field either chaotic or integrated.

If I take a deep breath and relax my energy field, then my input into our interactive field is quiet. However, if I'm anxious, I'm going to put disturbed energy into the field and that's going to disturb Helen's field.

Then she is going to react to being disturbed, which will in turn disturb my field. After a while, you don't know what is going on, other than you're both yelling at each other. That's because you're in a chaotic energy field. You need to learn to relax. Taking three to five deep breaths before you start talking is not just a meditative thing to do to meet the Eastern spiritual traditions. It is a practice rooted in physical science.

JUDY K. HERMAN

I can imagine a pool of water and the ripple effects being like an energy field. It makes sense that we affect each other's energy fields. Taking three to five deep breaths helps us relax before starting to talk. How does attitude affect the process?

HARVILLE HENDRIX

My attitude is equally, if not more, important when I'm dialoguing with Helen. If I feel negatively about Helen while I'm dialoguing with her, the negativity, even if it's not spoken, creates a chaotic energy field. My impact will be created with my tone of voice and the way I look at her. She can see whether my eyes are soft or hard, or if they have a glare or a gaze.

JUDY K. HERMAN

Even unspoken negativity creates a chaotic energy field. Tone of voice and facial expressions matter.

HARVILLE HENDRIX

If you want relaxation, you want to go into a gaze. You want the energy field to be cohesive and organized so you can talk about the problem. If we don't have an interaction that's free of the tension of the interaction itself, we will get involved only in the interaction. And we'll never be able to talk about the problem.

JUDY K. HERMAN

It's important to differentiate between the problem and the interaction itself.

HARVILLE HENDRIX

That's why there is structure in order to calm people down. The structure regulates the brain, so it's safe. If it's not safe, you're going to defend yourself and not solve any problems. If you're safe, you can be vulnerable and discuss and solve whatever problem you have.

JUDY K. HERMAN

Emotional safety sets the stage for you to be vulnerable in order to solve the real problem.

HARVILLE HENDRIX

For most couples, the problem is the way they interact with each other. So, they never get to the problem that produces this interaction. They just get caught up in the "you said this. . . no, I didn't say that. . . yes I did. . .I did close the garage door. . . no you didn't. . . I saw the garage door was open. . ."

It's the tone, not the content in those statements. The problem is the *way* it's said. So, the problem of closing the garage door gets ignored because the tone takes precedent.

JUDY K. HERMAN

With that kind of back-and-forth accusation and defensiveness, you lose sight of the problem.

HARVILLE HENDRIX

You can put any topic in that illustration including sex, money, children, time, vacations, or whatever. If there's tension in the interactive field, the tension will usurp the problem.

That's why dialogue became the intervention 30 years ago in Imago Therapy. We discovered that when couples connect, their problems tend to go away. The real problem was disconnection. When they connect, then they don't have that problem.

JUDY K. HERMAN

It makes sense that tension in the interactive field usurps the problem. The real problem is disconnection. Dialogue is the intervention that helps couples connect. For some couples, sitting across from each other and looking into each other's eyes is difficult. Looking into each other's eyes alone is powerful therapy.

Initially there can be so much tension in the counseling room. For some of the couples I've worked with, after a 90-minute session, they are able to embrace and look at each other with tears in their eyes. It's transformational. It's like no other therapy, really.

To me, it's like a sacred space that we're creating with three in the room. And I have the wonderful privilege as a therapist to see this transformation.

HELEN LAKELLY HUNT

You just said something that inspired me 25 years ago. Martin Buber, the Jewish mystic talked about the "I-Thou" in order for relationships to be healthy.[4] Most people treat others like an "I-it."

JUDY K. HERMAN

Please share more about this, Helen.

HELEN LAKELLY HUNT

For example, "you said you loved me the day we married. Well, if you love me, then you should agree with me. Don't I matter? If you loved me, you would do this for me. Or you would do that for me."

Buber says if a person lives with the other person being an "it," the relationship won't work.

If both treat each other like an "I-Thou," the universal energy of love moves into the space between the two people. It's sacred space. We believe there is something to the mystical. Nobody can answer where love comes from. It's a mystery. We know it shows up, however, when two people want to care about each other.

JUDY K. HERMAN

The relationship won't work if one or both treat the other with an "I-it" mentality. In my opinion, the "I-it" is really an illusion that we can control another person's life. On the other hand, if both treat each other with "I-Thou," then the universal energy of love moves into that space in-between the two.

How do you treat couples who have extra challenges such as a mental disorder or a neurodivergence? Does Imago Therapy help in those situations?

HARVILLE HENDRIX

It helps because in both of those instances and in many others, there is chaos and chaotic minds, dialogue is a structure that helps regulate the chaos.

The difference in working with anyone in a special situation is that the therapist must not assume they are an ordinary couple where there is a flow and an ease of understanding. You have to really slow down. Somebody might be able to mirror back only one word at a time. Or maybe five words or one sentence at time. That's okay. That's success.

JUDY K. HERMAN
Slowing down the dialogue process helps give structure to the chaos.

HARVILLE HENDRIX
Slowing down helps to integrate their brains. There's a high level of anxiety that needs regulation in order to function. Then they can begin to mentally improve using the structure, which is something they couldn't do when a high level of anxiety was present.

JUDY K. HERMAN
High anxiety can be regulated when slowing down. This helps integrate the brain and mentally improve.

HARVILLE HENDRIX
A therapist must be very mature and not assume their patient is like everyone else. They aren't like an ordinary car that you can get in and just drive. Instead, they are like a special car that requires you to know special things about it to get it to work.

There is no one for whom dialogue doesn't work. The brain is constantly on alert for something that will hurt it. All of us are a little bit paranoid. The brain doesn't automatically think others are nice. People don't automatically think others will treat them well.

The brain looks at even familiar faces and reads them. And if they see glossy eyes, they might think they need to be protective and defensive. The brain will always check to see if it is safe or dangerous.

JUDY K. HERMAN

This applies to all of us in addition to those with mental health challenges.

HARVILLE HENDRIX

The more chaotic the brain, the more it will assume it's in a dangerous place. It's already in chaos. Danger produces mental chaos because danger produces anxiety. And anxiety dysregulates the brain. If anything slows down the mental process, it's helping them breathe and making eye contact. Eventually they will reciprocate.

JUDY K. HERMAN

Helping them breathe and making eye contact invites them to feel safe.

HARVILLE HENDRIX

Many therapists say this can't work with special cases. Well, we don't know of anything else that works well with special cases. Everybody, no matter what, is looking to be safe. That's fundamental. When they are safe, they can connect with others. And when they can connect, they feel something different than being in danger and unable to connect.

JUDY K. HERMAN

With anxiety, there are deeper feelings of danger and disconnection. It's fundamental that everyone is longing to be safe and connected.

HELEN LAKELLY HUNT

A significant couple came to our *Safe Conversations®* [5] training which is the same thing as Imago therapy for those who want to impact others. Adrienne Kennedy who was the chair of the National Alliance of Mental Illness[6] participated. Then her husband, Hal Puthoff, [7] whose work is being nominated for the Nobel Prize in quantum physics also came to the training. Adrienne made this statement about the dialogue process. "If this was out into the world, this would end mental illness."

JUDY K. HERMAN

"If this was out into the world, this would end mental illness." That's a remarkable endorsement of how powerful the dialogue process is. Imago Therapy has also taken off in other parts of the world. Share about the international impact.

HARVILLE HENDRIX

We're in 62 countries now with about 2,500 trained therapists practicing in those countries. It's grown organically across the world.

JUDY K. HERMAN

Helen, did you ever dream of that when you first met, and you heard Harville talk about the stages of relationships?

HELEN LAKELLY HUNT

That's why I proposed. I hadn't heard anyone ever do something like this.

HARVILLE HENDRIX

I'm an academic who became a clinician and developed this system with Helen. I create systems.

JUDY K. HERMAN

Share more about how your book, *Getting the Love You Want,* became such a classic guide for couples.

HARVILLE HENDRIX

In the academic world when you publish a book, you count on 2,000 minimum or at the most, 20,000 people buying your book. Then it will go to paperback for a year. Then it will go out of print. I thought, because the book was about marriage, a popular subject, we might get two to five years out of it before it went out of print.

But what happened was, three weeks into the publication of the book we got a phone call from the producer at Oprah Winfrey. It may have done the normal run of 20,000, if we hadn't had a great marketer from the very start named Oprah Winfrey. On our first appearance on her show, there were about 20 million people watching.

JUDY K. HERMAN

That's fascinating to have such exposure!

HARVILLE HENDRIX

Two years later, we appeared on her show a second time. We were doing live demos in front of the camera. We did a whole workshop in front of the camera in her studio. People could see the clinical piece, instead of just hearing a description of what happens. People actually saw what happened with couples.

By the time that episode aired, her show was international. And 50 million people saw it. You can't even buy that kind of marketing. Judy, it was something I think you often say that it was divinely intended. So, Oprah is a part of the plan.

SUMMARY

1. Imago therapy brings structure to communication in order to create emotional safety and connection.

2. Dialogue is the intervention that calms the tension between two people as well as regulate mental wellness.

3. The more chaotic the brain, (as in mental illness) the more it will assume danger. Slowing down the breath and making eye contact invites safe conversations.

JUDY'S CHAPTER TAKEAWAYS

Harville and Helen are Legends! It was such a remarkable privilege to interview them even though I met them years ago, and they endorsed my book, *Beyond Messy Relationships*. It was rather magical for me to be in their presence. And if my imagination could talk, I felt the hidden "Oprah" in me at various times in our conversation. I felt proud to be a Certified Imago Relationship Therapist. And if my imagination were big enough, I'd believe that *Beyond Messy Relationships* could be included in Oprah's book club!

Given the depths of this interview, the written words don't even capture the light-hearted fun I saw with these two. When I referenced the quantum field of their playful energy, Helen reached behind Harville and gestured rabbit ears behind his head with her two fingers. You'll be able to watch it in your free toolkit: go to relationshipswithpurpose.com

 **Harville Hendrix, PhD and Helen LaKelly Hunt, PhD** are internationally respected couple's therapists, educators, speakers, and *New York Times* bestselling authors. Together, they have written over 10 books with more than 4 million copies sold, including the timeless classic, *Getting the Love You Want: A Guide for Couples.*

In addition, Harville has appeared on the Oprah Winfrey[8] television program 17 times! The pair are the co-creators of Imago Relationship Theory & Therapy, as well as Safe Conversations®, an organization that contributes to the creation of a relational culture through the distribution of new insights from the relational sciences.

TO CONTACT HARVILLE & HELEN

✉ https://harvilleandhelen.com/contact-us/

🔗 https://harvilleandhelen.com/

CHAPTER 11

HOW TO BE BETTER THROUGH ENNEAGRAM INSIGHTS

· · · · · · · · ·

Know Yourself
with Dr. Shelley Prevost and Dr. Chad Prevost

JUDY K. HERMAN

Chad and Shelley, as Enneagram practitioners, I am especially interested in your perspectives as an entrepreneurial couple. For people who know nothing about the Enneagram[1], would you explain what it is and why they should know about it?

DR. CHAD PREVOST

It's such a big system. Recently while walking with Shelley, I was talking about how much I love the Enneagram system, and how I wish I had known about it my entire life. When I look back, I realize how the Enneagram could have helped me know the people I worked with and know myself enough to know how I was engaging with others at different times.

The Enneagram is very versatile, and it can help in many different situations. This is perennial wisdom that comes from ancient sources. People can apply it to psychology, art, business, and relationships. It has improved the way people communicate with each other. It gives them shortcuts to self-understanding and to understanding others.

DR. SHELLEY PREVOST

Most people know that the Enneagram is a typology. It's a personality system that has nine different basic personality structures. Some people speculate that it's been around for thousands of years. It's originally based on some esoteric religious traditions.

There is a rich history of the Enneagram helping philosophers and thinkers understand universal truths. At its core there is a mathematical foundation. It's a framework for understanding the laws of the universe.

Then in the 1960s some psychiatrists and psychologists got a hold of it and realized it had a map for understanding personality development. During this time and into the '70s, the Enneagram began to take off in growth in psychology communities around the world. It came into the U.S. in the '70s and it's been going strong ever since.

There are more than nine personality structures. But when we work with people, we start with the nine basic structures to talk about their personality.

JUDY K. HERMAN

For our understanding, the Enneagram system can help couples and families communicate and understand each other better. Among its history, it starts with nine basic personality structures that aligns with ancient wisdom and universal laws.

With my exposure to the Enneagram, is it correct to say that it's like a lens in which people view the world and their relationships?

DR. CHAD PREVOST

Some people call it a lens. Different schools have different terminologies. The Enneagram is distinct from all other typologies, including Myers-Briggs.[2] The Enneagram is so incisive about looking at the motivations behind behaviors.

People can't assume someone else's type based on their behavior. They don't always know the underlying motivations behind others' actions. There are subtypes which includes three instincts and nine personalities. So that gives us 27 different personality types.

JUDY K. HERMAN

How accurate are the online Enneagram tests?

DR. SHELLEY PREVOST

People want to know what they are. I tell people it's one data point of the many dozen that can help them figure their type or help eliminate other types. I give a test through our program and that is probably the most accurate test out there. But it's still only one data point. People need to be on a journey of self-discovery. That is best done by reading, talking to people, and having a coach to guide you, who can point things out along the way.

Some people have an intrinsic seeker quality. The Enneagram can aid in that. People love talking about themselves. We love looking at ourselves and learning about ourselves even in shallow narcissistic ways.

Many people use the Enneagram to figure out who they are and what their personality is in order to get to the top. If we leave it there, that can be dangerous. Once people know their Enneagram type, the first step is to figure out their Enneagram personality. They can't just leave it at that. However, if they do, they are still in a box and still have limiting beliefs. They are still in their fixations and their unconscious emotional patterns. For example, I could say that I have a justification because I am a *Type Two*.

JUDY K. HERMAN

An online Enneagram test is just one data point. It's better to include reading, being in community and learning from a coach for more accurate understanding. Otherwise, the Enneagram system can be misused and even dangerous by keeping a person in their limited beliefs and fixations. They justify their "box" and are still unaware.

Share more about your beginnings as a couple and how the authentic growth track of the Enneagram system is helpful for relationships.

DR. CHAD PREVOST

We've been married for 23 years.

DR. SHELLEY PREVOST

We've been together for 25 years. And right when we got together, I was exposed to the Enneagram for the first time. I was getting my master's in clinical psychology when we started dating.

I was in this program and I asked Chad if he was willing to grow. Because I couldn't marry him if he wasn't going to grow. He told me he would grow, and then asked what that meant. It was important to me to have a partner who was pursuing personal and spiritual growth the way I needed to. At the time, the Enneagram didn't hook me like it has in the last five years. Now, it's become a shortcut.

When I used the term "growth" 25 years ago, I had a vague idea of what I meant. Now, it has become concrete to us using the Enneagram. As a *Type Two*, I will habitually struggle with certain patterns for the rest of my life. They're going to affect my spouse, how I parent, and how I show the things I'm not conscious of.

If I had a lens to use and the right language, the growth would have been more concrete and less vague and nebulous. I've been in and out of therapy for at least 25 years. And the ideas I learned with the Enneagram evaded me. They were too hard to understand. Since then, the Enneagram has given me a language for us to be able to talk about it.

DR. CHAD PREVOST

I had just finished seminary when she was beginning her counseling program. I concluded seminary with the feeling that I wasn't called to go into the ministry. I was casting about for what I was going to be. I wondered what my next authentic step was going to be. Like a lot of people, I resisted the therapy Shelley wanted me to do. I wasn't focused on it.

I thought I could accumulate the self-awareness and knowledge through learning more. That was a mistake. What I could learn was limited. We've had plenty of blind spots and a lot of work to do.

If I had known that I was a *Type Four* and she was a *Type Two*, that would have helped. We're both in the heart triad. We are both feelers. If I had known that my subtype is a person who is intense and expresses emotions readily, that would have helped so much.

JUDY K. HERMAN

In earlier stages of your relationship, you weren't drawn to the Enneagram. But you both wanted to keep growing in your knowledge and self-awareness. You just had your own ways of doing that.

Shelley, you're the helper, which is a *Type Two*. Chad, you're the romantic, which is a *Type Four*. Share more about this combination in your marriage.

DR. CHAD PREVOST

Type Four can be referred to as the individualist, or the romantic.

DR. SHELLEY PREVOST

Some people call it the artist. There are a lot of names for it. I was 20 and he was 23 as I was beginning graduate school and headed to Chicago. He had just finished seminary. We met at a youth summer camp where we both worked on staff. We were told there was a no dating policy. We didn't abide by that.

I thought he was cute and interesting. I wanted to figure him out. Because I'm a *Type Two*, I was less conscious of the patterns I repeat. I made a project out of him. I wanted to understand and help him dig into his mental and emotional self.

He's a *Type Four*, so he has a lot going on emotionally. There is a lot of complexity there. Because *Type Fours* are close to *Type Fives*. Both types are analytical. And I wanted to understand Chad.

DR. CHAD PREVOST

I could be intense and express myself socially in ways that had rough edges. That bothered Shelley. It's been a long 25 years working on those issues.

JUDY K. HERMAN

In your mid-20s you both seemed grounded, curious, and ready to grow on your own. Most of us don't know who we are or what we want at that age.

DR. SHELLEY PREVOST

I've always asked a lot of questions. Sometimes, as a child, I would get in trouble because I would ask too many questions. They weren't theological questions. But they were real questions I had when I was 7 or 8 years old. They were about things the church taught that I didn't understand. I would push back a little bit out of curiosity.

DR. CHAD PREVOST

A couple of years into Shelley's program, I was thinking about my next steps. Our dream was that she would be a counselor and I would a teacher. Before we got married, we were dreaming about holding retreats. We wanted to have a retreat center and create a program to help others in this missional way.

I got my PhD in creative writing to get a job as a professor. I was a professor for about a decade while Shelley was counseling. Then, we sidetracked into other professions and vocational experiences. Shelley was the CEO of a tech company and I worked in startups. The past couple of years we've been able to realize our dream of founding *Big Self School* together. Since the beginning of the pandemic, we've been working together.

DR. SHELLEY PREVOST

It was important for me to understand myself. It wasn't until the last five years, after I had a shock point, that my life began to break open. The poet Mark Nepo says, "We're either broken open, or we will fully shed[3]." That's the ego, the fixations, and these patterns.

I don't think I could have willfully shed anything. Life had to smack me in the face to realize that it was time for me to grow. It was time for me to take an honest look at patterns that haven't been serving me for my whole life. It's only now that I see the repercussions of those patterns. That's the power of the Enneagram. And that's what it's intended to do. No matter the age, most people stop their research once they figure out their personal type.

JUDY K. HERMAN

Both of you have a core that is dedicated to the inevitable growth that needs to happen. And whatever issues you have are mirrors to you as individuals. You two are modeling that growth individually and as a couple. Share more about the process of growth.

DR. CHAD PREVOST

I love the reminder Shelley just pointed out about how a lot of people will naturally resist typologies. We often hear people say, "I don't want to be labeled. I don't want to be put in a box."

The point of the Enneagram is to do the opposite. It's to help people unpack who they are psychologically, emotionally, and spiritually. Many people think they want to have a certain personality type. But every single type equally has their issues, their fixations, their passions, and their growth work to do. It's fortunate for me to have a partner who wants to grow. I'm glad Shelley has pushed me to grow and that she's been so dedicated to that.

DR. SHELLEY PREVOST

It really *is* a mirror. I'm growing because of Chad. Our Enneagram work as a couple has been interesting. Because I'm a two and he's a four, we share an inner line. Inner lines of the Enneagram are intimately connected. When I learned that, it felt obvious. There was a real unconscious pull to each other when we first met. Early in our relationship we read Harville Hendrix's book on Imago Therapy.

JUDY K. HERMAN

What I've learned as an Imago Therapist is that there is more to conflict than what is showing up in the moment. I see it now as an invitation to grow into your authentic self which I've termed a "divine invitation." We're designed to grow and grow up.

DR. SHELLEY PREVOST

The connecting point on the Enneagram that pulls us together also pulls us together in our shadow work. This work is not completely conscious, even now. For example, I was very critical and judgmental of Chad's actions because I did a

Facebook Live and was being critical of myself. Then I delivered my criticism to him on a silver platter. I was being snarky.

I asked myself, "What is going on with me?" It was all about my shadow stuff that I didn't want to deal with. Thank God I have partner who has grace and compassion. We can have a much better, richer, and more productive conversation instead of simply reacting to each other. I want to cry just thinking about it.

DR. CHAD PREVOST

It helps with reactivity and our natural gut impulse. For example, it's when Shelley named all of her pet peeves about me and little things that bothered her. At first, I tried to make light of it. But then she kept going. Then I started to feel bad.

Fours are famous for introjecting because, unconsciously, we are empaths. We absorb the feelings of those around us, whether they are good or bad. Now that I'm aware, I can choose not to introject that criticism. Even if it's still happening and I feel it, I can choose not to internalize it. That's part of the language and awareness we're able to have around our fights, even if they were only an hour ago.

JUDY K. HERMAN

Thank you for being vulnerable and allowing me to be part of this sacred moment just now as I experienced your deep emotion. I want people to know it's possible to be real and vulnerable. You two are so vulnerable for even putting yourselves in the hot seat on your own podcast. When I listened, I thought, "What married couple would do such a thing?"

Chad was there while Shelley was exposing her shadow stuff – the good, the bad, and the ugly – about herself. Chad was doing the same thing. It's one thing to do that for a therapist. And it's another thing to do it for someone else. But you two are hosting those moments for each other. I think that is remarkable. I want to honor that.

DR. SHELLEY PREVOST

We're just like every other couple. We're busy and we go through life. We shuffle kids around and cook dinner. On a good day, we do that for each other, even without the microphones. I am so grateful to have a partner who asks what's going on with me. He points out when I'm really on one.

We have foundation of curiosity. We both have the Enneagram system and deep love for each other. That makes our marriage stronger. He's my best friend, and I'm his. We've had a lot of growth and challenges. But, that's the good stuff. Our relationship isn't perfect at all.

DR. CHAD PREVOST

We haven't even talked about the fact that we work with each other. That adds a layer to things. Through the pandemic we were together a lot. Irritability shows up with too much togetherness.

JUDY K. HERMAN

This has been enlightening, beautiful, and encouraging. If you could give an entrepreneurial couple who is going through their own struggles some advice, what would it be?

DR. CHAD PREVOST

First, I would tell them to learn the Enneagram correctly.

DR. SHELLEY PREVOST

People should start with themselves. This was a hard lesson for me. When I feel triggered, reactive, or irritable, that's an invitation for me to slow down and check on myself. Then go outside of myself. It's difficult for me to do if I'm not practicing mindfulness and finding solitude. The big thing I would tell people is to start with themselves.

DR. CHAD PREVOST

That is the thing to take away. We can't do any better than that. In terms of working together, define your roles. That begins with self-awareness. Sometimes one person might care more than the other. And you must be able to communicate that and delegate so that it feels like an equal distribution of efforts.

SUMMARY

1. The Enneagram system can bring self-awareness psychologically, emotionally and spiritually in personal relationships.

2. Understanding each other's Enneagram number can increase empathy and personal growth.

3. Using the Enneagram correctly can help couples grow into appreciation and into mature ways of thinking which exposes their fixations and blind spots.

JUDY'S CHAPTER TAKEAWAYS

It touched me deeply to experience Shelley and Chad's tender and vulnerable moment in this interview. Their authenticity as a married couple is such a gift. Commitment to growth and partnership in learning the Enneagram shows us the value of this tool for greater insights in your primary relationship.

I appreciate Shelley mentioning that just knowing your number is not a place to land. Rather, it's a journey of continued insights and increased awareness of yourself and others. We can move out of reactive mode and into a conscious response. I may call it "psychological grounding."

When we have new insights, it's natural to wish you knew something years before and then wonder how it would have changed things. But I believe that the timing of what we know is exactly when we are supposed to know it. We all need grace for the humanness of our younger selves.

For your free toolkit go to relationshipswithpurpose.com

Chad Prevost is an author, publisher, coach, and certified Enneagram practitioner with advanced degrees in creative writing, literature, and theology.

He's participated in writing and literary arts communities in New York, Austin, Atlanta, and Chattanooga and now spreads his passion for the Enneagram throughout the Southeast.

Shelley Prevost is a licensed therapist, educational psychologist, leadership coach, and Enneagram practitioner.

She has 25 years of clinical and coaching experience combined with spending over 10 years as a business coach and startup executive who helps leaders be their wisest and most authentic selves.

Both Chad and Shelley are the Co-founders of the Big Self School supporting the mental and emotional wellbeing of leaders through coaching, consulting, events, and a podcast.

TO CONTACT CHAD & SHELLEY

✉ https://www.bigselfschool.com/contact

🔗 https://www.bigselfschool.com/

CHAPTER 12

HOW TO GET THE HELP YOU NEED

•••••••••

Explore Coaching and Counseling
with Dr. Robin Buckley

JUDY K. HERMAN

As mental health professionals, there are reasons we choose this profession. Share *your* story and how you became a both a psychologist *and* a coach.

DR. ROBIN BUCKLEY

I've always wanted to be in a profession that helps people. That likely came from parents who emulated that. My dad was a teacher working in disadvantaged communities. My mom was a nurse. They exuded this idea of giving beyond yourself.

It was a natural alignment to choose psychology. I went into the mental health field to support people. Once there, I discovered it's more often focused on crisis intervention. I was raised to be proactive, take charge, and try to prevent problems before they happen.

Around the time I finished my doctoral degree, I discovered coaching. Still in its infancy as a profession, I was trained as a coach. I was working with people who want to make changes, not just because they are in crisis. It resonated with me because they wanted a better life, relationship, or career.

I believe people can be empowered to take charge of their lives in a way that works best for them. It was a great alignment between my education, cognitive behavioral strategies, and my training as a coach.

JUDY K. HERMAN
It's amazing that you discovered coaching early rather than later in your career.

DR. ROBIN BUCKLEY
I finished my PhD in 2001 and coaching certification in 2005. The idea of learning and expanding always appeals to me. A lot of my colleagues made fun of me for becoming a coach because I had my doctoral degree. I didn't know that over time, people would start seeking out coaches.

JUDY K. HERMAN
Many of us therapists take pride in having the initials behind our names. We work hard for those initials. Yet, being a coach doesn't require standardized training or certifications.

DR. ROBIN BUCKLEY
Even over the last several years I could feel the term "coach" catch in my throat when I use the word. I'm much better now. Part of the stigma comes from the fact that there are areas of coaching that aren't regulated.

Coaches don't have to be licensed like therapists and psychologists. Anyone can call themselves a coach with or without training. That made me pause and ask if I wanted to align myself with a field that anyone could get into.

Instead of getting stuck on that, I decided to embrace the idea that I could be an effective coach; especially with my educational background and training. I love to educate people on how to work with the right coach. They need to know what a coach's training and background is.

One of the most important pieces of coaching is that you can't just teach people based on your personal experiences. A lot of untrained coaches make the mistake of thinking that since they've been through something, they can teach others about it. That shouldn't be the intention.

JUDY K. HERMAN

I agree that coaching people based on a coach's experience alone is not enough. Rather, structured or even standardized training is important. How did you discover your passion to help high-achieving women and couples?

DR. ROBIN BUCKLEY

I wanted to work with girls and women since college. I was raised by a very strong mom who was adamant that I had a career to support myself, even if I ended up getting married. She was very pragmatic and really encouraged my sister and I to take charge of our lives.

My mom trained me to think about how to help and support women. She taught us that women needed to get past ridiculous stereotypes that are outdated. I always gravitated toward working with women. There is something special about helping other women reach their goals. My book, *Voices From the Village*: *Advice for Girls on the Verge of Adulthood*[1] came from my passion of helping women.

I found that with women executives and business owners, in almost every case, their relationships came up as hindrances or just another challenge in their lives. I regularly heard about their relationships.

As I worked with them, I started to think of a different approach to helping couples. Their relationships were impacting these people individually. So, I wanted to get to the root of the problem. The more I thought about it, the more I started expanding. I began to offer my individual clients the opportunity to explore their relationship through coaching.

My training in cognitive-behavioral strategies applies both to business and to helping couples. On a personal note, I've been married more than once. This is ironic since I help people with their relationships.

JUDY K. HERMAN

If you were to imagine your younger self and you hired yourself as who you are now, what would you have done differently? What would you have experienced as your younger self?

DR. ROBIN BUCKLEY

By working with me, my younger self would have had a strategic plan on how to choose a partner or how to explore my options for partners. If I was already in a relationship, my coaching would have created a solid platform for that relationship based on love instead of sexual attraction.

I would have had a long-term plan for where I wanted the marriage or commitment to go. As a younger woman I didn't have any of those things. I went with what I felt. It's not wrong, but it might not get you the results you're looking for. You should base your relationship on the long-term goal of staying in a committed relationship and not only on your subjective current experiences.

If I had been able to work with someone when I was younger who had the same coaching method I do now, I would have been able to think about things pragmatically, strategically, and objectively. You can still have all the bells and whistles, all the fun, a lot of sex, and love all the good stuff. It doesn't take it away. Having an objective plan makes sure the bells and whistles have a platform to continue to be positive.

JUDY K. HERMAN

A strategic plan for a romantic relationship makes sense. I like the idea of the bells and whistles having a platform to continue. This is like the structure or the framework you would have for building a house. When is the best time for a couple to begin coaching in order to build that framework? Is your program a good fit for both individuals and couples?

DR. ROBIN BUCKLEY

I work with a lot of uncoupled people who don't want to make the mistakes they made in the past. They want a secure strategy of how to have a relationship. Some of the work I do with couples is applicable to people who are single.

For example, I work with individuals to develop their ICA. In business, an ICA is an ideal customer or client avatar. People who are looking to get into a relationship create an ideal companion avatar. It's still an ICA with the same idea. It makes you examine who you really want to be with. They go through a structured questionnaire, and we have conversations about the type of partner they are looking for.

JUDY K. HERMAN
An ICA is an "ideal companion avatar."

DR. ROBIN BUCKLEY
You must know what kind of relationship you are looking for. Otherwise, you might not align with who you *think* you want to be with. I help people develop this idea, so they have a plan when they are out in the dating world. When they decide to spend time with an individual, they know if that person is fun for the moment or someone who fits everything they're looking for.

People shy away from this because they hear the words strategy and plan. I use these business terms and they think it sounds too manipulative. But it's not manipulative in the negative sense. It's manipulating the type of life they want.

Society has twisted the term. Manipulation is not always a negative thing. Sometimes it's just manipulating a variable to reach your goals. If you're not hurting anybody, having a plan for your life is okay.

When I work with individuals or couples, it's all about building that solid platform. Couples come in to work with me for two main reasons. I work with couples who are at the brink of making a commitment. And I work with couples who have been married for a long time and are in a rut.

They're not in crisis because *that* should be talked about in therapy. They just want to feel better in their relationship. They want to be with their partner just as satisfied and happy as they used to be.

JUDY K. HERMAN

Building a solid platform and having a plan for your life can help a person be more aware as they make crucial decisions. How does a couple know if they need a therapist or a coach?

DR. ROBIN BUCKLEY

There are some clear categories that should start in therapy. If there is any kind of addiction, recent abuse, a traumatic loss, or a recent affair, those couples should seek out therapy.

I've worked with couples who had infidelities in their past, but it's not an issue anymore. The people who are still raw from an affair should go to therapy. Those issues need to be addressed at a therapeutic level.

There is a delineation between therapy and coaching that should not be overlapped. People who feel they need to dig into their past issues, analyze, and talk about them, should start in therapy.

One of the clear differences between therapy and coaching, is that coaching is not covered by insurance. On the other hand, not all counseling practices take insurance either. That may be a factor for some.

The clearest difference beyond the logistics is that therapy is going to spend more time looking at the past to make changes in the present. Coaching looks at your present and how you want your present to be. It also looks at how you are going to use what you are doing in the present to get to the future.

Coaching is a very progressive forward-looking approach to achieving the relationship you want.

JUDY K. HERMAN

That's a clear description between coaching and counseling. In counseling, you'll spend more time clearing away the past to make positive changes in the present. Whereas coaching is more progressive and forward-thinking.

Some clients want to go back to how it was in the past.

DR. ROBIN BUCKLEY

When couples tell me they want to be back to where they were, I ask them if that's what they really want, and if so, why? They can't get back there because that's 10 years ago. And now, they're different people.

Now we're creating a relationship based on who they are now, and on the relationship they want in the future. Some people might say that's semantics. But I'm trying to help couples and individuals understand *their* focus and what *they* want to do. If someone has clinical issues like depression or anxiety, then they *should* be working with a therapist who can manage their big picture perspective.

JUDY K. HERMAN

A therapist can help clients manage their big picture perspective. Do you ever take on clients who are seeing therapists individually but come to you because they want to move forward together as a couple?

DR. ROBIN BUCKLEY

I do. Therapists and coaches deal with separate issues in a person's life. If couples come in and there's still something clinical, they are seeing a therapist about, then coaching can help facilitate their work in therapy. Then the work they do in therapy facilitates the coaching.

JUDY K. HERMAN

It can be very complementary with the right coordination of people supporting you. And it takes a village for a marriage to thrive.

On another note, how has your work changed you and your perspective about life?

DR. ROBIN BUCKLEY

When you ask, "How has my work changed me?" I realize I'm not *just* teaching and supporting people by using cognitive behavioral strategies and good coaching strategies. I do it now almost automatically in my life.

That doesn't make my life perfect by any means, but it helps me be more effective, which makes me more satisfied with my life. I want to help my clients get to a level of confidence with the ability to do hard things. I want my clients to avoid using services that might become a crutch, which can happen with therapy.

JUDY K. HERMAN

In other words, we want clients to outgrow their therapy. As practitioners, it's important to model growth and resilience for clients. The 50 or 60 year-old self has the capability of a mature perspective that the 22 year-old self couldn't have. This is a human journey to grow and grow up.

Share more about your coaching modality.

DR. ROBIN BUCKLEY

My approach is based on a business model. I frame it by using very specific business terminology and business concepts.

For example, I may ask a very driven Type A couple to tell me about their mission statement. They each start rattling off their mission statement at work and why their business has one. Then I tell them I was asking for a mission statement for their relationship.

They each turn to the other and ask, "Why don't we have a mission statement for our relationship?" They know all the reasons why an organization has one. It keeps people focused, on the same page, and working towards a mutually accepted goal.

Those all sound like good things to have in a relationship. We start there and then we expand using parts of an actual business plan to create the plan for their relationship. When couples are done with the work, they walk out with a copy of their specific relationship plan.

I don't dictate their goals. I help them identify their pain points. Framing it this way, with objective terminology and concepts, helps couple retain their pragmatic and logical way of thinking rather than getting caught up in their emotions.

All the emotions that are associated with relationships are

lovely, wonderful, and necessary. But emotions can cloud our thinking. We can't come up with the best new approaches when we are *only* emotional. I try to help couples strip it down to the business of their relationship, then we create a plan that will work for them.

JUDY K. HERMAN

I can see how that is tailor fit for high-performance couples. I encourage my clients to consider emotions as temporary messengers to their soul. If depression and anxiety come, listen to them, and honor them. Let them show you their message and zone into that deeper place. Tune your soul into the messages. Thank the emotions for showing up with the messages. And then let them go. Even if the emotion is anger or irritability, there is a message there.

It's great that your model helps couples get down to their framework without emotions being in the driver's seat of their relationship.

DR. ROBIN BUCKLEY

I had fun developing the program and watch how couples truly start to embrace it. I love seeing couples use the terminologies we talked about. So many therapy sessions are about actions one person in the couple does that the other hates.

In coaching, we help the couple retain their objectivity by using business phrases. Their ability to create plans, long-term goals, and define roles allows them to be successful as a couple. We don't do that in our relationships, even though for many of these couples, they do it very effectively in one area of their life. They get to translate what they do well into their relationship. It doesn't take away from the love, lust, and all the fun stuff. It enhances it.

JUDY K. HERMAN

What do you say to couples who think that coaching is too expensive for them?

DR. ROBIN BUCKLEY

In the work I do, we use quantitative evidence. We can see if we're achieving the goals just like a business would.

For those who question the investment, I'll ask them how much they spent on their wedding. By the way, the average wedding in the United States costs $20,000. Then I ask how many hours they spent planning their wedding? The average American spends 250 to 300 hours in wedding plans. Then I ask how many hours or how much money they've spent on their marriage. It's another one of those moments where I hear crickets.

So, I ask, "If you spent $20,000 on a wedding for an eight-hour day, how much is it worth to create a solid foundation for your marriage and what you want for your future?" That's when the couple realizes it's worth coming to coaching. Some people come in once a week, some come in once a month. It depends on their process and how fast they want to progress. Is it worth spending 12 hours in weekly meetings for three months in order to get the foundation you want for you marriage? I hope so.

It's important for people to get their relationship on a reestablished track they want for their future. Our brains function in a very back and white way. When we use numbers and percentages, people start to understand the value of couples coaching. Then they make the decision that is right for them.

JUDY K. HERMAN

Do you compare the cost of coaching to the cost of a divorce?

DR. ROBIN BUCKLEY

I have worked with couples who are going into their second or third commitment or marriage. They are scared and don't want to go through a divorce again. It's not just the financial aspect. It easily costs $12,000 to $20,000 to get a divorce which take on average 18 months to finalize. That's on the plus side.

It's not just about the time and money of a divorce. It's about what the divorce does to you. It's about the thoughts you create about yourself and about your ability to be in a relationship. The typical divorce process can undermine a person to their core.

Sometimes they question their values, judgement of others, and who they thought they were. If you knew you could avoid a physical injury by doing something, you would do it. If I don't jump off the roof of my house, I will avoid breaking my leg. It's not that different from coaching.

If you want to avoid the pain of a divorce, wouldn't you do things that are preventative? Wouldn't you want to ensure you will have success in your relationship and avoid that pain? We make plans in other areas in our lives to avoid getting hurt. We normally don't see it as much in relationships.

JUDY K. HERMAN

In our work with couples, we're not just working with the couple and their problems. Instead, there's healing and changes that trickle down to their families. Couples in coaching or counseling have the potential of changing their family trees. How does having a structure and a plan affect the entire family?

DR. ROBIN BUCKLEY

I've had previous couples who gave their adult children sessions with me as a gift. They want their kids to have the same kind of plan and strategy in place.

JUDY K. HERMAN

What about couples who have a hard time dealing with extended family or ex-spouses?

DR. ROBIN BUCKLEY

The term we use is "collaterals." Those are all the people outside of the couple. The couple is the nucleus. We ensure that the couple is strong and unified because they have a ripple effect out to everybody else.

For example, if a spouse won't stand up to their ex, the other spouse may feel as though their partner is always choosing the ex. That's a clear pain point. My goal is to help them reestablish that they are a fused unit. And the ex is collateral and will stay collateral.

It revolves around creating plans for your collaterals, just as you would create plans for your teams in business. Each team might need different strategies. It addresses if your team is good or bad, and whether it's going to affect the leadership. In this case, it's going to affect the nuclear couple. There are plans and ways to organize the collaterals to benefit the relationship.

JUDY K. HERMAN

Using business strategies in your relationships makes a lot of sense. Labels can be empowering. It helps couples to know their collaterals, their assets, and their liabilities. It's their team and their core they are fighting for.

DR. ROBIN BUCKLEY

It takes away the emotion. When we talk about the ex's or the kids, different emotions come up. Emotions are messages, but they are messages to process and let go of.

Talking about collaterals are as neutral and clinical as you can get. It takes away some of the heartstrings that get pulled when thinking about our kids or others in the family. Collaterals are neutral. The sole purpose of the couple is to figure out how to work the collaterals and interact with them so that it doesn't hurt the relationship. Maybe it will even benefit the relationship.

JUDY K. HERMAN

Is there one piece of advice that you would give to a high achieving woman who has outgrown her marriage and has tried everything to make it work?

DR. ROBIN BUCKLEY

First and foremost, take time to clearly articulate and write down what you want. Don't write what you need, what you should be doing, or what you should have done. Instead, think about what you want out of your life and relationships.

If you write it down and research it, it becomes real. Then review it. Until your brain accepts it, you have a reminder talking to you from the page. Once you establish what you want, know that it's not selfish.

This is the strongest most selfless thing you can do. Your happiness and satisfaction come through, which creates a ripple effect to everyone you know. Then you can make choices around what you want. Whether you want a relationship where you feel supported, or you don't want to be in a relationship because you want to be independent, you can use your research as litmus test for the choices you make.

JUDY K. HERMAN

You just gave beautiful advice for women to write down what they want.

SUMMARY

1. Coaches don't have to be licensed like therapists and psychologists. Since anyone can call themselves a coach, it's important to know they have additional training.

2. In counseling, you'll spend more time clearing away the past to make positive changes in the present. Whereas coaching is more progressive and forward-thinking.

3. Writing down what you want is the strongest most selfless thing you can do because your happiness creates a ripple effect to everyone you know.

JUDY'S CHAPTER
TAKEAWAYS

Dr. Buckley brings us great clarity about the distinction between couples counseling and couples coaching. If you were in the fog about this before, you likely know what you're ready for now.

I normally help couples define their core values together in a Relationship Vision. This is the first time I've thought of a business plan model to structure a relationship. It makes sense to neutralize high-intensity emotions around the "collaterals" and focus on the kind of partnership you really want.

I have used analogies of deposits and withdrawals in reference to interactions couples have with each other. But it's even more potent to label the "liabilities and assets" and be intentional about your partnership in life!

For your free toolkit go to relationshipswithpurpose.com

Dr. Robin Buckley, CPC, has a PhD in clinical psychology and served as a doctoral professor and dissertation chair for students in business, leadership, education, and healthcare. She is an author, public speaker, and cognitive-behavioral coach who works with executive women and high-performance couples as well as a columnist for Entrepreneur.com.

Dr. Buckley is the founder of Insights Group Psychological & Coaching Services. Her proprietary coaching model uses a business framework and cognitive-behavioral strategies to support clients in creating and executing concrete, strategic plans for developing their careers and relationships.

TO CONTACT DR. BUCKLEY

✉ drrobin@insightsgroup.com

🔗 https://drrobinbuckley.com/

NOW WHAT?

Wow! Talk about compelling conversations! If you're like me, you're grateful for the knowledge, experiences, and passions of each guest featured. These interviews were filled with amazing insights. It's not just beneficial information about various issues, but it's a wealth of wisdom to digest with potential for real and lasting change.

So, how do you feel after reading this book?

Not only do I hope you're inspired, I invite you to take a deep breath of fresh A.I.R right now. Remember the acronym I mentioned a few times? **Awareness, Intentionality,** and **Risks of growth?** Yes, breathe again and ask yourself.

- *How am I now more Aware?*
- *What Intentions do I have after reading this book?*
- *What is my Risk of growth right now?*

For example, you might say, "I'm now more **aware** of what a long-term relationship needs. I **intend** to make a plan for my next right steps. My **risk of growth** is to download the free toolkit and share with a friend."

To get the toolkit, go to:

RELATIONSHIPSWITHPURPOSE.COM

Or you may **intend** to go back to the chapters with the particular guests that resonated with you. Your **risk of growth** may be to reach out for support or access *their* resources.

THERE'S ANOTHER STEP YOU CAN TAKE.

Because you've gotten this book, you're entitled to a complimentary Clarity Call. This is a time for me to listen and help give you clarity on your next right steps. I'll answer any questions you have, and I may even answer ones you didn't think to ask.

If you'd like to get your Clarity Call scheduled, or just ask me a question, go here:

RelationshipsWithPurpose.com

My intent is to show that you're not alone. You have what it takes to create a better relationship and a better life.

The fact that you are reading this now means two very important things.

First, you resonated with the content enough to continue reading to the end. I'm grateful for that, because it's my intention to support you right where you are.

Second, and most important, it shows that you value your relationships and your life. And you're committed to making both your life and relationships better. Since this book featured couples, you may be thinking about your spouse or partner. But your relationships can be better with your children, your parents, or your friends. Or you can improve a professional relationship with your colleagues, employees, or your bosses. Having better relationships and a better life will play a critical role in virtually every season and circumstance you encounter.

There may have been times when you read something and said, "I didn't know that." If so, I hope the next thing you said was, "I can do something about that."

So, let me ask the question which is the title of this section. Now what? Now that you have this information, how do you get the most out of what you've learned? How do you create momentum for what you know in your heart is *your* next right step?

Better relationships lead to a better life. Isn't that what you deserve? I would love to hear from you and support you on your journey.

Share your Relationships With Purpose Success Story at

RelationshipsWithPurpose.com

NOTES

Introduction

[1] Groundhog Day (film) - Wikipedia. (1993, February 4). Retrieved from https://en.wikipedia.org/wiki/Groundhog_Day_(film)

Chapter 1 How to Create Long-Term Love & Flow

[1] Hendricks, G., & Hendricks, K. (1992). *Conscious Loving: The Journey to Co-Commitment.* Bantam.

[2] Hendricks, G., & Hendricks, K. (2016). *Conscious Loving Ever After: How to Create Thriving Relationships at Midlife and Beyond.*

[3] Herman, J. K. (2019). *Beyond Messy Relationships: Divine Invitations to Your Authentic Self.*

[4] Hendricks, K. Somatic Therapy for Problems in the Relationship Dance. ISSSEEM Magazine, Vol. 7, No. 1, 7-11, Spring 1996. *ISSSEEM Magazine.*

[5] Oprah Winfrey - Wikipedia. (2018, January 1). Retrieved from https://en.wikipedia.org/wiki/Oprah_Winfrey

[6] Erik Erikson – Wikipedia. (2016, January 1). Erik Erikson – Wikipedia. https://en.wikipedia.org/wiki/Erik_Erikson

[7] Hendricks, G. (2021). *The Genius Zone: The Breakthrough Process to End Negative Thinking and Live in True Creativity.* St. Martin's Essentials.

[8] Gospel of Thomas - Wikipedia. (2016, September 1). Retrieved from
https://en.wikipedia.org/wiki/Gospel_of_Thomas

[9] Seminars - Hendricks Institute. (n.d.). Retrieved from
https://hendricks.com/seminars/

[10] Hendricks, G. (2010). *The Big Leap: Conquer Your Hidden Fear and Take Life to the Next Level.*

Chapter 2 How to Respect Long-term Differences

[1] Coaching - Official Site Dan Miller. (2019, January 18). Retrieved from https://www.48days.com/coaching/

[2] Mennonites - Wikipedia. (2022, January 1). Retrieved from https://en.wikipedia.org/wiki/Mennonites

[3] Miller, J. F. (2016). *Creating a Haven of Peace: When You're Feeling down, Finances Are Flat, and Tempers Are Rising.*

[4] Miller, D. (2003). *The Rudder of the Day: A 48 Days Devotional.*

[5] Read Some of Barbara Bush's Most Memorable Quotes. (2018, April 18). Retrieved from
https://time.com/5244413/barbara-bush-most-memorable-quotes/

[6] Miller, D. (2010). *48 Days to the Work You Love: Preparing for the New Normal.*

[7] Miller, J., & McHugh, D. (2014). *Be Your Finest Art.*

Chapter 4 How to Love Stronger Through Severe Mental Illness

[1] Lukach, M. (2017). *My Lovely Wife in the Psych Ward: A Memoir*. Harper Wave.

[2] Understanding Psychosis. (n.d.). Retrieved from https://www.nimh.nih.gov/health/publications/understanding-psychosis

[3] Hallucinations: MedlinePlus Medical Encyclopedia. (n.d.). Retrieved from https://medlineplus.gov/ency/article/003258.htm

[4] Kiran, C., & Chaudhury, S. (n.d.). Understanding delusions. https://doi.org/10.4103/0972-6748.57851

[5] What Is Mania, and What Does It Mean to Have a Manic Episode? Here's What Experts Say | NAMI: National Alliance on Mental Illness. (n.d.). Retrieved from https://www.nami.org/Press-Media/In-The-News/2021/What-Is-Mania-and-What-Does-It-Mean-to-Have-a-Manic-Episode-Here-s-What-Experts-Say

[6] Bipolar Disorder. (n.d.). Retrieved from https://www.nimh.nih.gov/health/topics/bipolar-disorder

[7] Schizoaffective Disorder | NAMI: National Alliance on Mental Illness. (n.d.). Retrieved from https://www.nami.org/About-Mental-Illness/Mental-Health-Conditions/Schizoaffective-Disorder

[8] Mental Health Video Resource Library | NAMI: National Alliance on Mental Illness. (n.d.). Retrieved from https://www.nami.org/Support-Education/Video-Resource-Library/What-is-Schizophrenia

[9] Anosognosia | NAMI: National Alliance on Mental Illness. (n.d.). Retrieved from https://www.nami.org/About-Mental-Illness/Common-with-Mental-Illness/Anosognosia

[10] Amador, X. (2020). *I Am Not Sick I Don't Need Help! How to Help Someone Accept Treatment - 20th Anniversary Edition.*

[11] Lithium (Oral Route) Side Effects - Mayo Clinic. (n.d.). Retrieved from https://www.mayoclinic.org/drugs-supplements/lithium-oral-route/side-effects/drg-20064603?p=1

[12] Herman. (2020). Dance of Mental Illness. In *Beyond Messy Relationships: Divine Invitations to Your Authentic Self.* United States: Morgan James.

[13] Lukach. (n.d.). Out of the Darkness. *https://www.nytimes.com.*

[14] The Atlantic. (n.d.). Retrieved from https://www.theatlantic.com

[15] Lukach. (n.d.). My Lovely Wife in the Psych Ward. *https://psmag.com.*

[16] Nast, C., & W. (n.d.). WIRED - The Latest in Technology, Science, Culture and Business. Retrieved from https://www.wired.com/

Chapter 5 How to Live Better, Even with Distractions

[1] Homepage - Judy Herman. (n.d.). Retrieved from https://www.judycounselor.com/

[2] Attention-Deficit/Hyperactivity Disorder. (n.d.). Retrieved from https://www.nimh.nih.gov/health/topics/attention-deficit-hyperactivity-disorder-adhd

[3] Orlov, M. (2010). *The ADHD Effect on Marriage: Understand and Rebuild Your Relationship in Six Steps.*

[4] Getting a Diagnosis | ADHD and Marriage. (n.d.). Retrieved from https://www.adhdmarriage.com/treatment_guide/diagnostic-advice

[5] How to Improve Treatment of ADHD in 3 Steps | ADHD and Marriage. (n.d.). Retrieved from https://www.adhdmarriage.com/content/how-improve-treatment-adhd-3-steps

[6] Exercise is Great Treatment for ADHD | ADHD and Marriage. (n.d.). Retrieved from https://www.adhdmarriage.com/content/exercise-great-treatment-adhd

[7] How Mindfulness Can Help Deal with Adult ADHD | ADHD and Marriage. (2016, January 28). Retrieved from https://www.adhdmarriage.com/content/how-mindfulness-can-help-deal-adult-adhd

[8] Non-Medicinal Treatments for ADHD | ADHD and Marriage. (n.d.). Retrieved from https://www.adhdmarriage.com/treatment_guide/non-medicinal-treatments-adhd

[9] ADHD, Bipolar, or Both? What You Need to Know | ADHD and Marriage. (2016, August 19). Retrieved from https://www.adhdmarriage.com/content/adhd-bipolar-or-both-what-you-need-know

[10] How ADHD affects relationships and what to do about it | ADHD and Marriage. (n.d.). Retrieved from https://www.adhdmarriage.com/event/how-adhd-affects-relationships-and-what-do-about-it

[11] Orlov, M., & Kohlenberger, N. (2014). *The Couple's Guide to Thriving with ADHD.*

[12] What's the Difference Between ADD and ADHD? | ADHD and Marriage. (n.d.). Retrieved from https://www.adhdmarriage.com/content/whats-difference-between-add-and-adhd

Chapter 6 How to Build Better After Betrayal

[1] Growth After Trauma. https://www.apa.org/monitor/2016/11/growth-trauma. (n.d.).

[2] About PBT - The PBT Institute. (n.d.). Retrieved from https://thepbtinstitute.com/about-debi-6/about-pbt/

[3] Post-Traumatic Stress Disorder. (n.d.). Retrieved from https://www.nimh.nih.gov/health/topics/post-traumatic-stress-disorder-ptsd

[4] Silber, D. (2020). *Trust Again: Overcoming Betrayal and Regaining Health, Confidence, and Happiness.*

[5] Silber, D. (2021). *From Hardened to Healed: The Effortless Path to Release Resistance, Get Unstuck, and Create a Life You Love.*

[7] Silber, D. (2017). *The Unshakable Woman: 4 Steps to Rebuilding Your Body, Mind and Life after a Life Crisis.*

[8] Podcast - The PBT Institute. (n.d.). Retrieved from https://thepbtinstitute.com/podcast/

Chapter 7 How to Heal Better Beyond Addictions

[1] Capparucci, E. (2021). *Going Deeper: How the Inner Child Impacts Your Sexual Addiction: The Road to Recovery Goes Through Your Childhood.*

[2] Inner Child Recovery Process - Eddie Capparucci. (n.d.). Retrieved from https://abundantlifecounselingga.com/inner-child-recovery-process-for-sex-porn-addiction/

[3] https://www.drbarbarasteffens.com. (n.d.). Retrieved from https://www.drbarbarasteffens.com

[4] Post-Traumatic Stress Disorder. (n.d.). Retrieved from https://www.nimh.nih.gov/health/topics/post-traumatic-stress-disorder-ptsd

Chapter 8 How to Live Happily Even After

[1] Thomas, K. W. (2016). *Conscious Uncoupling: 5 Steps to Living Happily Even After*. Harmony.

[2] Young-Eisendrath, P. (2019). *Love Between Equals: Relationship As a Spiritual Path.*

[3] Books | Stephanie Coontz. (2011, January 4). Retrieved from https://www.stephaniecoontz.com/books

[4] About Fuller. (2021, August 11). Retrieved from https://www.bfi.org/about-fuller/

[5] Ahrons, C. (1998). *The Good Divorce*. William Marrow Paperbooks.

[6] Gilligan, S. G. (1997). *The Courage to Love: Principles and Practices of Self-Relations Psychotherapy*.

[7] Stephen Covey - Wikipedia. (2020, June 9). Retrieved from https://en.wikipedia.org/wiki/Stephen_Covey

[8] John & Julie Gottman - About | The Gottman Institute. (n.d.). Retrieved from https://www.gottman.com/about/john-julie-gottman/

[9] Thomas, K. W. (2010). *Calling in the One: 7 Weeks to Attract the Love of Your Life*. Three Rivers Press.

Chapter 9 How to Extract Clarity from Emotional Abuse

[1] Patrick Doyle | Get Free From Emotional Abuse. (n.d.). Retrieved from https://www.patrickdoyle.life/

[2] Hoffman, N. (2018). *Is it Me? Making Sense of Your Confusing Marriage: A Christian Woman's Guide to Hidden Emotional and Spiritual Abuse*.

[3] Definition of MISOGYNISTIC. (2023, February 22). Retrieved from https://www.merriam-webster.com/dictionary/misogynistic

[4] *Bill Gothard - Wikipedia*. (2018, May 22). Bill Gothard - Wikipedia. https://en.wikipedia.org/wiki/Bill_Gothard

[5] Home - Leslie Vernick. (n.d.). Retrieved from https://leslievernick.com/

[6] Townsend, J. (2004). *Who's Pushing Your Buttons?: Handling the Difficult People in Your Life.*

[7] Vernick, L. (2013). *The Emotionally Destructive Marriage: How to Find Your Voice and Reclaim Your Hope.* WaterBrook.

[8] What to Know About Complex PTSD and Its Symptoms. (2021, April 12). Retrieved from https://www.webmd.com/mental-health/what-to-know-complex-ptsd-symptoms

[9] Borderline Personality Disorder. (n.d.). Retrieved from https://www.nimh.nih.gov/health/topics/borderline-personality-disorder

[10] *Flying Free Sisterhood Program.* (n.d.). Flying Free Sisterhood Program. https://www.flyingfreesisterhood.com/sign-up

[11] The Flying Free Podcast - Expert Interviews, Survivor Stories, and More. (n.d.). Retrieved from https://www.flyingfreenow.com/flying-free-podcast/

Chapter 10 How to Create Connection Beyond Conflict

[1] Hendrix, H. (2005). *Getting the Love You Want: A Guide for Couples.* Pocket Books.

[2] Imago Relationships. (2021, October 3). *Imago Relationships Worldwide - Imago Relationships.* https://imagorelationships.org/

[3] Siegel, D. J. (2012). *Pocket Guide to Interpersonal Neurobiology: an Integrative Handbook of the Mind (Norton Series on Interpersonal Neurobiology)* (Vol. 0).

[4] I and Thou - Wikipedia. (2008, March 1). Retrieved from https://en.wikipedia.org/wiki/I_and_Thou

[5] Conversations, S. (2023, March 1). What is Safe Conversations - Safe Conversations. Retrieved from https://safeconversations.com/what-is-safe-conversations/

[6] NAMI's New President Outlines Priorities for Serious Mental Illness | NAMI: National Alliance on Mental Illness. (n.d.). Retrieved from https://www.nami.org/About-NAMI/NAMI-News/2018/NAMI-s-New-President-Outlines-Priorities-for-Serio

[7] Harold E. Puthoff - Wikipedia. (2023, January 5). Retrieved from https://en.wikipedia.org/wiki/Harold_E._Puthoff

[8] Oprah Winfrey - Wikipedia. (2018, January 1). Retrieved from https://en.wikipedia.org/wiki/Oprah_Winfrey

Chapter 11 How to Be Better Through Enneagram Insights

[1] Enneagram of Personality - Wikipedia. (2023, February 1). Retrieved from https://en.wikipedia.org/wiki/Enneagram_of_Personality

[2] The Myers & Briggs Foundation - MBTI® Basics. (n.d.). Retrieved from https://www.myersbriggs.org/my-mbti-personality-type/mbti-basics/

[3] Mark Nepo – spiritual writer, poet, philosopher, healing arts teacher, cancer survivor. (n.d.). Retrieved from https://marknepo.com

Chapter 12 How to Get The Help You Need

[1] Buckley, R. (2016). *Voices from the Village: Advice for Girls on the Verge of Adulthood: Instructor's Guide.*

Made in the USA
Columbia, SC
07 September 2023

22552914R00152